Making Progress

By

Brady Moller

Copyright © 2017 by Brady Moller

All rights reserved. No part of this publication may be reproduced, distributed, or transmitted in any form or by any means, including photocopying, recording, or other electronic or mechanical methods, without the prior written permission of the publisher, except in the case of brief quotations embodied in critical reviews and certain other non-commercial uses permitted by copyright law. For permission requests, write to the publisher, addressed "Attention: Permissions Coordinator," at the address below.
brady@eyesofanaddict.com

Editor: Tony Smith
Graphics: GraphicPunch

Please be sure up to my mailing list for email on free books and upcoming promotions:

Sign up here!

Dedication

For: Magda Moller

Mom, thank you for being my rock. Every time I think about how far we've come, a wave of emotion floods over me.
Against all odds, we've come out stronger than ever.
Thank you for always having my back.
I couldn't have wished or asked for a better mom and for that, I'm eternally grateful to the universe.

Love you, mom!

Table of contents:

INTRODUCTON	5
PART ONE – SELF DISCOVERY	8
An introduction to self-discovery	9
Life is one big chess game	11
The power of acceptance	16
Why negativity can be good for you	20
Asking for help	23
Trust issues – a means of manipulation	27
How to focus on your own trauma	30
Mental and physical elasticity	32
PART TWO – ADDICTION	36
Introduction to addiction	37
What is addiction?	39
Signs of addiction	43
The addict that does not want help	53
Dealing with an eating addiction	57
Dealing with a shopping addiction	68
Dealing with a gambling addiction	76
PART THREE – LIFE'S LESSONS	85
How to deal with life's disappointments	86
How to forgive and forget	101
Understanding and dealing with resentments	106
Jealousy – a sign of insecurity	112
Loneliness	116
The value of a smile	126
A compliment a day	128

About the author   Making Progress
                                    131

INTRODUCTION

Sitting on the corner of the street, the perpetual fumes from his old, unwashed clothing block his nose. Any sense of smell he once had, is lost. Many things he has lost in this cruel nightmare called life. His greatest loss of all, dignity. He has become immune to the smell that drives off thousands of people a day; often holding their noses as they try and get away with as little eye contact as possible. Eye contact means they might have to engage with this man and that is the last thing they want.

The 6am traffic rush is about to start and he knows it's time to get ready. It's going to be another long day of work. His job is not ideal, but it's all he has. Anything short of this job and he will probably starve. Hey, at least he hasn't turned to crime. Not yet, at least.

He feels the cold draft enter his body through the bottom of his shoes (shoes a size or two too small), but it beats wearing nothing at all).
His black feet have hardened and serves as a protective layer from the scorching tar in the Summer. In this instance, it serves as a protective layer against the icy draft that enters through the worn-out soles of his shoes.

There aren't many perks to his job. The greatest would probably be that he works from home – a perk so many wish they had.
To make a living, he scrapes ice from a tin he uses, that reveals the words, "Please, Help." and "God bless you."

Business is booming as more and more cars start congesting the roads. The coins in his tin rattle as he shakes it and begins begging for money. The cold makes rattling the tin much easier than normal.

"Get off the fucking road," *a voice shouts.* "It's because of fuck ups like you, that this country is where it is today. Get a job, lazy ass." *The screaming man continues.*

The homeless man realized that asking this angry man for money is a futile exercise and continues walking.

By now, he's used to such comments. These comments don't affect him anymore.

They almost don't affect him anymore.

A problem that many of us have, whether it's on a conscious or subconscious level, is that we believe in a system of hierarchy. People fit into different classes of life. Someone will always be higher or lower than the next.
Many people stand in admiration of major business leaders and CEO's of large corporate companies, because we view them as *accomplished.* We respect those that have a higher position than us, even if it is only to their face.
We read about stories of success or bravery and think of these people as heroes. Now I don't want to take away from the successes of any of these accomplished individuals. But, what if we were to view the homeless man on the street with that same level of respect?

Okay. Let's stop there.

You're probably reading this and thinking to yourself, *Yeah, that's a sad story. But, what does this have to do with me? I bought this book because I want to discover myself and learn how to deal with MY problems.*

This book is written for you to help discover who you are and for you to learn how to deal with life's most difficult challenges. Here's the thing, if we are to grow, we need to be willing to look inside of ourselves. We need to be willing to acknowledge and accept where we are wrong, what areas we can improve on and where we are willing to grow.

Self-development is not a selfish process.
Why do I say that?
Because none of us were born into this world alone. If we are ever to succeed at this challenge called life, we need to look inside of ourselves and learn how to appreciate those around us. Appreciate those in the same way that we would like to be appreciated, that we would like to be treated.

If you are **unwilling** to dig deep and realize where you might be wrong, which areas of your life can do with major improvement, and see how a simple change in mindset can benefit your life, then sadly, this book is not for you.

If you want to better yourself, develop a healthy mindset and realize that your happiness does not solely depend on **you**. Then, I'll be ecstatic that you could join me on this journey of self-discovery.

In this book, you can expect the following:

1. *Discover where we fit in the grand scheme of life*
2. *Understand our roles in this world*
3. *Learn to adapt a total mindset shift when looking at our problems*
4. *Learn why acceptance can be one of your most powerful tools*
5. *Common mistakes made by many when trying to work on their emotional issues*
6. *The effects of avoiding our issues*
7. *How the global disease of addiction affects us as well as the consequences of not addressing our issues*
8. *We will be digging deeper in some of the most common behavioural addictions*
   Why these addictions exist,
   How to help others with the disease of addiction and
   How to recover from them.
9. *An in-depth understanding of some of life's most complex problems and how to work through these issues. This includes: forgiveness, resentments, loneliness, disappointments, and jealousy*
10. *Finally, we will look at two very simple, yet practical ways to ensure a happier, more positive you - starting from today*

Food for thought:

How would you like others to respond to your pleas for help if the positions were flipped and you had to stand in the icy cold, begging for money?

Let us begin.

PART ONE – SELF DISCOVERY

CHAPTER ONE

An introduction to self-discovery

Life is hard. It's meant to be that way.

If life were easy, we wouldn't have any lessons to learn. We wouldn't know what sadness feels like, and in turn, we wouldn't appreciate the feeling of happiness.

For us to appreciate the feeling of happiness, we need to understand what it feels like to be sad or angry.

If life were easy, then solving life's problems would be easy too.
I think we can both agree that this is NOT the case?
Most of life's problems worth solving is much harder than we would rather have. For us to truly and comfortably answer some of life's greatest mysteries, we need to be willing to dig deep.
Much deeper than we could have imagined.

This applies to all our problems. We cannot simply focus on the *problem* itself, we must be willing to unravel and discover what the root cause of our problems are.

I know this may sound a bit confusing now, so let's illustrate what I mean with the below example.

Brady has a problem being honest. In fact, he has found that his constant lies are only working to his detriment.
The more he lies, the more unmanageable his life becomes.

So, to fix this, he read a book about positivity and decided to put what he learned into practice.
He wakes up every morning and makes positive self-affirmations. He makes a conscious decision to try his hardest to be honest!

"Just for today, I will be honest! Just for today, I will be honest!"

Here's the thing, I can declare my honesty until I am blue in the face. I might be honest for a few days, but eventually, I will lie again.
Why?
Because I have only focused on the **problem**, rather than focusing on the **cause** of the problem.

The problem is that I'm constantly being dishonest. The problem is quite clear. Identifying a problem won't take that problem away; it's but the first step of working on any problem. What really matters is the **underlying reason behind** my dishonesty.

Once we identify the reasons behind our actions, only then do we begin working on our problems.

1. Was I perhaps scared to tell the truth? In other words, is the reason behind my constant lying fear based?
2. Was I worried about what people might think of me if I were to tell the truth? Is my pride holding me back from speaking my truth?
3. Was I scared that I would be rejected if I spoke the truth?

The reality is, lying is not the problem. Lying is the defense mechanism. The real problem is the reason **why** I lie. Only once I start addressing those crucial, underlying issues do I start addressing the problem.

The first part of this book is dedicated towards understanding where we fit in the grand scheme of life. No two people are the same, we all have our own roles to play, each with their unique mannerisms.

Before we can start working on ourselves, we need to gain a better understanding of *who* we are: what makes us tick, what we enjoy most, where our weaknesses lie, our fears and our strengths.

Once we have this understanding, we can then establish what areas in our life we need to work on.

CHAPTER TWO

Life is one big Chess game

Chess is a strategy board game where all the pieces move in different positions. Each piece has its own strengths and limitations and are moved to strategically over-power the opponent's King, this is how the players win the game.

Life is one big Chess game.

In this game of life, every decision we make has an impact on the rest of your game. One bad move and your entire game could be ruined. Some bad moves aren't that crucial and they are easier to recover from.
The key to the game of Chess, is not to focus on the wrong moves already made, but rather to focus on the moves you still have available to make a difference. You cannot undo your moves, but you can move forward.

Each game of Chess consists of 32 initial pieces.

2 Kings
2 Queens
4 Rooks (Castles)
4 Knights
4 Bishops
16 Pawns

From the above, it's obvious that not all pieces are equal. In the game of Chess, there are:

The few elite.

The powerful reinforcements.

The free spirits.

The majority – dedicated hard workers.

At first glance, it would appear as though some of those pieces are *lucky*. From the onset, they have been placed in positions of power, without having to do *much* work.
Other pieces have to work hard if they have any hopes of "moving up" in life. The majority of pieces fall into this category.

Life is one big chess board. All the pieces represent each type of person in this world.

I don't want to bore you with the specifics of the game, but the point that I'm trying to make is that each of these pieces represents us and where we have been placed in this world.

As I have mentioned, I firmly believe that self-discovery is an intertwined journey. It's therefore crucial that we understand, not only where we fit, but the roles other people play in our lives as well.

The King

These are the all-powerful influencers and the decision makers. They don't move around much, but they have a huge following. They are well protected by all the other pieces and are generally protected at all costs. All the other players on the board move in the interest of these all-powerful Chess pieces.

Examples of the Kings in the real world would include:

> *Donald trump, Adolf Hitler, celebrities, royalty, large corporate CEOs, etc.*

What's interesting to note with these all-powerful pieces is that even with all their power, if the "kings" in real life do not have substantial backup from those around him, they are almost useless.

These powerful beings are only as powerful as all the other pieces allow them to be.

The Queen

The most powerful piece of all, with unmatched freedom of movement.
You cannot deny that the queen holds a lot power, but with all this power, try as she might, the Queen will always only be second to the king.

Examples of the Queens in the real world would include:

> *Expert politicians, Heads of different governmental sectors, managers, directors of big corporations, etc.*

The Queen has a lot of influence, but if she is not careful, she may easily be replaced by an upcoming pawn. Much like the King, as powerful as the Queen may be, she is almost useless without the support of the other pieces on the board.

The Bishop

These players stay on their own color. They can move around as much they like, provided they do not move away from their set colour.

Examples of Bishops in the real world would include:

> *Conservative or traditional people that generally try sticking to rigid regime, etc.*

These "pieces" avoid change at all costs and prefer to remain in their comfort zones. These pieces are crucial to the King's success and often serve as loyal Devotees.

The Knights

These players represent those that love freedom!
They move around the world with their heart on their sleeve. They are the motivators of the world. Those that encourage change.
Like all other pieces, their positive attributes can lead to their downfall as well. They do not always follow rules or suggestions.

Examples of the Knights in the real world include:

Nelson Mandela, Priests, Freedom fighters, activists, positive thinkers, etc.

What's interesting to note is their free-spirited capabilities are so unique that not even the Queen can perform these moves.

The Rook (Castle)

These pieces are tall, head-strong, and powerful.
Their almost intimidating power is often used to fight off the bad and protect all the other pieces on the board. These pieces provide support to the rest of the pieces.

Examples of Rooks in the real world include:

Army, police force, firefighters, etc.

Pawns

The workers.
The most overlooked, yet crucial pieces in the game of life. Without pawns, the "higher powers" would be weak.
The all-powerful often use these pieces for their own gain. The pawn stays headstrong and looks ahead, knowing that if they work hard enough, they will get rewarded.

Sometimes, the pawn becomes so fixated on moving up, that they lose themselves in the process…

Most of us fall into this category…

Again, what's interesting to note is that if the pawn has made it to the other end of the board, they are "promoted" and can become any other piece, besides the King.

In this game of life, you cannot just focus on your next move. You must focus on your next *three* moves. The next move you make has an impact on the moves you're allowed to and will be forced to make in the future.

Every decision you make today will have an impact on your future decisions tomorrow, regardless of where you fit in this game of life.

Sometimes we make decisions fully believing it was our best, but it ends up being the worst decision we could have made.
What's important is how fast we are willing to get back up and start again. Each piece must keep moving.
Mistakes are made and learned from.
Such is the game of life.

In the game of life, which chess piece best describes you?

This chapter may seem largely insignificant, but it's important to know our role in life. With this knowledge, you know how to plan your next move.

It's crucial for you to identify your strengths and weaknesses.
The aim of this chapter was to help you initiate a thought process that drives you to think about what your capabilities and limitations are.

CHAPTER THREE

The power of acceptance

So, here's a little bit about me.

In the game of life, I've identified myself as a knight.
Free spirited and I generally hate sticking to rules.
I carry my heart on my sleeve and I'm a firm believer in *being the change I want to see.*
But as with every other piece in the game, I have my shortfalls.
Not following rules has caused me to land in a great deal of trouble.
I had my fair share of trials, but eventually, after years of emotional suppression, I turned to drugs, alcohol, gambling, and sex, amongst many things, to try and *numb* myself. My free-spirited nature got the better of me.

Now this is not a memoir of any kind, so I don't want to spend too much time talking about myself.
What I do want to focus on, is my journey in recovery.
It was during this journey that I learned the value of one of the most powerful tools.

Acceptance.

As it turned out, I had a skewed perception of *acceptance.*
I viewed acceptance as a sign of weakness. Acceptance would mean that I'm openly admitting I'm powerless over something. That I just let it happen.

Many of us have this perception.

When I first started my journey in recovery, I was told that acceptance is key to dealing with my addiction problem.
Scratch that.
Acceptance is key to dealing with **any** problem.
What I later realized, is that acceptance is not simply the act of acknowledging a problem and then pretending it doesn't exist, but rather that acceptance is the first step to solving any problem.

If you find yourself struggling to come to terms with something or accepting a situation (be it physical, financial, or emotional), I want you to try this little trick I learned.
Simply add the phrase, *"for now,"* after everything we *"accept."*
Before you go on reading, quickly, try it.
Think of a difficult situation that you are currently faced with, something that you would rather pretend doesn't exist.

Perhaps you are unhappy with your life, or you hate the fact that you don't know how to handle money. Perhaps you've gained a lot of weight and you feel really shitty about it.

Just think of any problem area that is currently affecting you, and *know* you need to accept.
Now say it out loud.
Sucks hearing it out loud, doesn't it?
Now say it again, but this time, include the words *"for now!"* Put emphasis on those last two words and let it sink in.
Doesn't that sound so much better?
It could feel like a weight has been lifted off your chest. Perhaps you even feel worse. If you do, just know that this is only temporary, because soon you will start working on changing it. The power is all in those two little words.

Have you noticed how we have already started changing our mindset and how we have started looking at things differently?

It is important to realize that **acceptance** and **tolerance** are two completely different things. Often people confuse the two.

Acceptance is accepting my reality as it is now. That is, at this very present moment in time.

Tolerance is recognizing what I dislike, or what I wish were different in my life and doing nothing to change it.

Consider:
*I **accept** that I have a very low self-image and think very little of myself, **for now.***

Let's understand why acceptance is important using the above example.

Lesson 1

Acceptance is not a sign of weakness.

In the above example, I have accepted my current "weakness," and admitted that I do not think highly of myself. This is not a sign of weakness, this is the first step to dealing with the problem.
By accepting, you become aware and acknowledge that it is there. On the contrary, this is a sign of strength. Wouldn't it be easier for me to just avoid my problem and pretend as though it doesn't exist?
I have identified a soft spot, something I would much rather pretend didn't exist. That, in itself, is difficult.
Without acknowledging the problems we have that need to be addressed, we won't have anything to *fix.*
The process of acceptance is understanding that nothing can be done to change the past, but we can start working on fixing our current problems or difficulties because of our past, to ensure a better future.

Lesson 2

Acceptance does not make you powerless.

I believed that by *accepting* something, I became powerless over whatever I'm accepting.
We may not always be able to do things or have things the way we want, but that shouldn't be confused for being powerless.

Even in scenarios where we *accept people for who they are,* we are not powerless. We still have choices and we can still choose how we react to those people, what boundaries we put in place or our view of these people.

Don't confuse acceptance for being powerless. Once again, acceptance is an act of understanding and acknowledgment of our CURRENT situation.

Lesson 3

Acceptance is only useful when followed up by healthy, self-loving actions.

Refer back to the ***for now*** lesson.

The key to acceptance is not beating ourselves up. The key is to view this as a positive an enlightening experience, one that will help us grow and learn from.

Acceptance can be a powerful life tool, but without healthy actions that need to follow, it can be useless, or worse, harmful.

CHAPTER FOUR

Why negativity can be good for you

He lays in his bed watching sad videos on YouTube. He desperately wants to cry, but he can't. Somehow, he feels that if he cries and lets out all his frustration, life would be better.
People all around him are happy and the mere sight of this makes him angry. He's tired, alone, and scared. Everyone around him can see it. He's just too much of a coward to admit it to himself.

All self-help books and articles on the web emphasize on one driving character trait – **positivity.**

When we're in a positive state of mind, we become grateful. We develop a brighter outlook on life. Hell, we even start looking for the good in people we previously didn't like.
With enough positivity around, life becomes one big frigging positive ball of happiness.

But, what happens when all that positivity fails you and you start breaking down? What happens when life has thrown us so many curve balls that even the most seasoned Gurus lash out or break down?

Here's a harsh little truth:
Life doesn't always play out as we might have hoped.

We might have lost a loved one.
Perhaps we're angry at ourselves or someone else.
Maybe our attempts at being helpful and maintaining this *positive attitude* only slapped us in the face?

Despite all our efforts to maintain a positive attitude, we have only experienced hurt and pain. People start taking advantage of us, they start using us, they know they can get away with it…
I could go on with all the potential things that people could do to dampen our spirits, but what I'm trying to get at, is that it is not always practical for us to be positive. In fact, it's unrealistic.
Sometimes, we have no other option, but to be miserable, upset, or angry.

The power of negativity

Because of everything we've been taught, people avoid negativity like the plague. Negativity will only do us more harm than good. It brings on nothing but bad vibes and energy. For this reason, we fake smiles, we try to still be that good person everybody wants us to be. At the end of the book, we will explore the power of smiling. But, at what point does positivity do more harm than good?

Unexpressed emotions find a way to escape.
The longer we suppress them, the worse the after-effects will be when they do eventually surface.

This chapter is dedicated to the power of negativity and how your negativity can help drive a positive attitude.
Now, I know, you may be thinking, *Wait! I thought this isn't another chapter on positivity!?*
I'm sorry to inform you, but it is.
That's just the thing. Even in negativity, there is positivity.

Take a second to think about some of the best moments you've lived through. Think of the smiles and happiness associated with those times.

Now ask yourself the question, what makes those moments so memorable?
What made this the happy moment that stood out for you?
It's those moments of negativity that made the moments of positivity so special.

Let's use a simple example to elaborate:
David comes from a very wealthy family. He's so wealthy that he often doesn't know what to do with his money.
One day, he is gifted with 10 thousand bucks from some random, unknown source.

Sure, this may make him smile a bit, but what's the chances that he would have the same feelings of relief as opposed to someone that: has been without food for three days, has no place to sleep, and no family to turn to?

Because the homeless guy has been in such a bad space financially, he would appreciate the money a lot more than David would.

Our negativity can be amongst the most powerful emotional tools we have to help us realize what's really important to us.

Negativity is really positivity in disguise. It readies us for those good, happy moments. It makes us appreciate and treasure these moments.

Instead of avoiding or running away from negativity, embrace it. It's really just there to amplify our happy moments when they do eventually arrive.

It's okay not to feel okay. Negativity is really just positivity in disguise.

Now that's a comforting thought, isn't it?

CHAPTER FIVE
Asking for help

"Oh my God, I can't do this anymore" he sobs.

"Help!" Whispered, so softly that he could barely hear the desperation in his own voice.

Let's not beat around the bush, **asking for help sucks.**

It's one of the hardest things to do. I'm not just referring to a person in recovery or a person with an illness or character flaw. This applies to all seemingly "strong" individuals.

Before we ask for help, let's look at the people offering it.

Very often, we don't even need to ask for help!
It could be starring us right in the face, but still, we would politely decline and continue our suffering. The saddest part of all, is that most of the time, these people are sincere when offering the help and genuinely are extending a much needed helping hand.
I can think of so many people that have offered me help and in fear of coming across as weak or helpless, I would usually say, "No thank you, I'm okay."
What made matters worse, is that I would then sit in my self-pitiful state, believing I was all alone in the world.
I would feel incredibly helpless, even though I just foolishly declined the help that was freely offered to me because of my own insecurities.

We often turn relatively simple problems into complex multi-layered problems just because we struggle to accept help.

Asking for help

Asking for help is very hard for a lot of us, yet, there are often so many times that we don't even need to ask for help.

Just think to a few of these times. A loved one approached you and asked if you're okay, or if there's anything they can do for you? Your pride got in the way and you politely decline, assuring them that you are in fact okay.

I think it's clear most of the time, we don't even need to reach out and ask for help. It's there already, we just refuse to take it. This is because we either believe that we can do everything on our own or our pride gets the better of us.

Now, we are not always so fortunate to be offered help and it gets to the point when our desperation gets so bad that we are left with no option but to ask for help.

You often hear people saying, "Asking for help is one of the biggest acts of humility."
What does this mean!?
Let's not kid ourselves, asking for help can be very risky.
What makes the act of asking for help soo humbling is that you stand at the risk of all of being rejected, the fear of appearing to be lazy, weak, incompetent. The shame and embarrassment that could possibly follow.

"Ugh!!!! It's all horrible! You know what?! Screw it. I'm sure I can do it myself!"

The humility involved goes a bit deeper than the more obvious points listed above.
Asking for help is an act of humility, because it is understanding and accepting that I cannot do everything myself, that I am not the superhero I have subconsciously made myself out to be.

I had to learn to ask for help, otherwise all the other personal development tools I have learned would become fruitless. This is a lesson I learned and it's a lesson I would like to share with you as well.
For you to progress emotionally, learning to ask for help when needed, is a must.

So, I started asking for help because I realized that if I did not do so, I would be holding myself back from the personal growth I might have made.
For me to achieve great things, I sometimes needed help and that's okay.

Now that I realized that my inability to ask for help was holding me back from achieving the emotional freedom I sought. This was something I would have to overcome.

I soon realized that I was not asking for the help because I wanted to, I was merely complying and asking for help because I was "forced" to. Secretly, I did not see the value in it. I did not see why humiliating myself and admittedly confessing, "I was weak" would help.

That's when it clicked.
For me to ask for help and truly benefit from it, I need to first see or understand the value in asking for help.

It was only when I started realizing and seeing the value in asking for help that I understood why asking for help is so important and just how much it can benefit, not only myself, but the person I'm asking the help from.

When we help others, we do it, not only for that person, but for ourselves as well. Whether this is on a conscious or sub-conscious level, we get satisfaction out of helping others.
By helping others, I feel good about myself, knowing that I did something to leave a positive impact on another person.

Discovering the value in asking for help is not easy, especially when it's not something you're used to doing.
Please, don't expect this to be an easy task. It's often hard to change a behavior that you have become so accustomed to.

Try to avoid doing what I did.
Instead of seeing it as something that must be done, see this as a new skill you're about to learn. With all skills, practice makes perfect. The more you practice, the easier it becomes and the more value you see in other people helping you, where you cannot help yourself.

So, the first step was to realize that I would not be able to achieve asking for help successfully overnight and that it would probably take a lot of practice. Little victories and a lot of feelings of shame, embarrassment, and discontent I have associated with asking for help over the years.
Those temporary feelings are something I have accepted.

Secondly, I had to assess why it was so incredibly difficult for me to ask for help. Like I mentioned in the beginning of this section, for all problems, we need to dig deeper to truly find what the underlying problem is.

The problem wasn't me asking for help, the problem was all the negative associations I had with asking for help.

If asking for help is something that you struggle with, I want you to take a quick break and use these few moments to think about some of the possible reasons behind why this may be a problematic area in your life.
Try digging deep. Think back to your childhood. Think of what you associate *asking for help* with. Think of any fears that come to mind.
Once you're done, I'll share you with my personal reasons behind my fears in asking for help.

Personally, I struggled to ask for help, because as a child, I often felt that it was my place to be seen and not heard.
I had a very lonely childhood and was often left to my own devices, so doing everything on my own became the norm.

Once I identified these underlying issues, I realized that I would need a mindset shift for me to successfully learn the art of asking for help.
So, I started off small. It was very difficult, sometimes even stuttering as I found myself asking for help. But, I knew that I would indirectly start addressing my childhood issues and that made it worth it.
I would ask for help with small things and simply observe the response. The responses varied. Often people were more than willing to assist when they could. Other times, people couldn't assist, and that was okay too.

Please, please, please, don't treat this task as a means for you to get out of doing things for yourself. Help should only be called on when you realize that you cannot do something by yourself.

CHAPTER SIX

Trust issues as a means of manipulation

There's something about this guy though, she thinks to herself.
"You know you can trust me, right?" She begs of him. Her eyes, ever so intrigued.
"Please don't take it personally, but I don't actually trust anybody. I can tell you this much though, there's a very good reason why I don't trust most people."
"I understand, one day you will finally trust me, I can tell you that much."
He grins uncomfortably.

I have had issues with trusting people for a large part of my life. Growing up, I was very secretive about a lot of things. My best friends wouldn't even know what was going on in my head at the best of times.

Secrets keep you sick. Mine kept me safe. I grew up fully believing that I was protecting myself by not revealing too much to anyone.

Much like asking for help, trusting people would also require a great deal of vulnerability. If I trusted someone enough to let them in, I would have to reveal who I really was and not the person I would prefer the world to see (after all, the world would never like me for who I really am, right?).
I carried this train of thought with me throughout my childhood, into my teenage years, and into adulthood.
Carrying secrets built up from so many years can become taxing on any person.

I had to let go of these secrets. Letting go of all these secrets would be a very freeing experience.

That was the problem!
It was freeing.

What I did not quite realize that I was doing at the time, I was manipulating people into staying into my life with my "trust issues."
Let me explain.

I became this vortex of mystery. A puzzle that was so enticing to others. A puzzle that had to be solved.

With the people that were closest to me, I would always be "a part" of the group, but I came with a certain air of mystery.
What I would do, is let people in slowly - bit by bit. I would give them a piece of the puzzle, but never enough pieces to fully solve this mysterious puzzle.
My closest friends held onto these pieces, trusting, and believing I would one day give them enough pieces to figure me out. All they need to do is prove they are trustworthy enough.
Needless to say, I never revealed the puzzle and a large part of my life remained a mystery to them.

In my defense, I never realized what I was doing until I embarked on my journey of emotional freedom.
I never fully let anyone in because in doing so, I manipulatively kept that person in my life and "interested."

Admittedly, it came as a shocking revelation and reflects to what extent I would go to try and keep people in my life. After speaking about this revelation, I also found that I am not the only person who has done this. Like myself, they weren't fully aware that they were using their trust issues to keep people in their life either.

Other people also use their trust issues to try keep other people at bay. Their trust issues are used to ensure people don't get too close.
This way, you get to "build" relationships with other people, but if and when the relationship turns sour, they feel less hurt.

Many people suffer from trust issues. In fact, it is completely normal to not want to allow every Tom, Dick, and Harry into your personal life.
When you start using your trust issues as a means of manipulation, that is when it becomes unhealthy.

Take a few seconds to think about your own trust issues.
Have you used these issues to keep people in your life?
Have you used these issues to keep people at bay?
Are you able to identify the reasons behind your actions?

CHAPTER SEVEN

How to focus on your own trauma

The concept of trauma has been a troubling one for myself and probably many others. What I have found, is that people often compare trauma to that of others. They grade their traumatic experiences based on other's experiences. By doing this, they never truly pay their experiences the attention it deserves.

This may sound a bit confusing, so let's break it down.

What is trauma?
Very simply, trauma can be described as a deeply disturbing experience, resulting in pain. Be it physical or emotional, there will always be pain.

We often compare our own painful experiences to that of others.
Let's look at an example to illustrate what I mean.
John was robbed of his cell phone at gun point.
Cindy was molested as a child by her uncle.
Based on the above, both are terrible and painful, but who had it worse off? John or Cindy?

If you answered either John or Cindy, you're wrong.
That is because John cannot compare his experience to Cindy's and vice versa. Both experiences are traumatic to *that* person, and comparing either experience would not be fair.

The risks with comparing our traumatic experiences to that of others:

1. We minimise our own experiences

2. We feel guilty about feeling bad, because we believe that our experiences are incomparable to other's.
3. We end up feeling sorry for ourselves, believing that we go through the most difficult, trying times, while others have it easy.

I have been through a few unpleasant events myself.
I would then think of someone else's pain, someone that may *seemingly* have experienced a much deeper pain.
I then use this to remind myself of the *gratitude* I aim to one day achieve and therefore *realize* that my problems aren't actually that bad.

If I must be completely honest with myself…am I being grateful or am I merely using the pain of other's as a deflection for me not have to deal with my own pain?

Trauma = Pain, and pain will be felt. No matter how hard we try running from it. It may not happen right away, but eventually, it will be felt.

Trauma cannot be compared. What may be traumatic for me, may not be traumatic for you.

One thing I have come to learn and realize is that we cannot run from our past. We may find many ways to hide from it, but eventually (**and it always does**), our past will come back to haunt us.

We need to address our own traumatic experiences. If we avoid dealing with these experiences, they will define who we are. Our trauma will define our behaviors and our defense mechanisms. Often resulting in us lying, hiding, struggling to trust people, difficulty asking for help, and all other fear-based actions which is often revealed in numerous forms, be it aggressive, vengeful, pitiful etc.

Trauma manifests itself in various ways and differs from person to person. What is constant is that un-dealt with traumatic experiences almost always results in negative character defects.
These defects of character become our norm – they become our defense mechanisms.

The sooner we deal with our trauma, the sooner we begin to heal and experience that sought after feeling of self-content.

CHAPTER EIGHT
Mental and Physical Elasticity

Regardless of who we are, we all have problems.

Problems have to be dealt with.

I KNOW! It sounds like I've been preaching the same thing over and over again, but that's because it's super important! In the next section of the book, we will start uncovering some of the effects of us failing to deal with our "problems."

I was in an AA meeting not too long ago, and someone said, "I feel like an elastic band."
At first, I didn't quite understand what that meant. Not knowing bugged me. So, I went home and really gave it some thought and then it suddenly hit me.
Elasticity is the ability of an object to return to its normal state once pulled or stretched.

An elastic band has the ability to be pulled, stretched, and disfigured. Once you let go of the elastic band, it returns to its *seemingly* normal state.
At first, it appears as though the elastic band is restored to its normal state, but the more wear and tear the band has, the less elasticity it has.

Most elastic bands are made to withstand a certain amount of pulling and stretching, anything more than what it is designed for has a negative impact on the elastic band.
The longer the elastic band is stretched, the less elasticity is has. Furthermore, elastic bands can be pulled, stretched and so forth multiple times, but eventually, it reaches a point where it cannot handle all the pressure.
The elastic band snaps.

This *elastic band theory* inspired the final chapter in this section of self-discovery.

<u>People are like elastic bands.</u>
We naturally come with the ability to be moulded.
There are countless examples that could illustrate this.
Think of how we go to work or school every day. We take on different roles and wear different masks to perform whatever tasks required, when we return home, we get to unwind and relax. *We return to our normal state.*
Think of how we deal with heartbreak after a relationship has ended. When we're alone, we grieve, but as soon as other people surround us, again, we return to our *normal state.*
We learn different languages, we experience different emotions, we make new decisions every day.
The point that I'm trying to make is that people are naturally born with the ability to change.
We're naturally born with elasticity.

We are like big, breathing, elastic bands.
There are forces that control our elasticity though. In life, these forces are the decision makers, and they lead us to be stretched further or to be bent in different ways.

Like elastic bands, people come with a certain threshold. There is a limit to how far we can be stretched or pulled to maintain our elasticity, anything after that causes unnecessary tension and could even cause us to snap.

When we are in a healthy state, we can handle the forces that stretch and pull us. These are healthy forces and it's what our bodies are capable of.
Our problems are the forces that pull us, that over-stretch us.

In this final chapter, I want to emphasize the importance of dealing with our problems. Understanding **why** our problems need to be dealt with is crucial before getting into "how to guides" later.
Often, we manage to get away from our problems. We pretend as if they don't exist or we try burying them, in the hopes that we may forget about them.
Our problems always come back and when they do, they bend us a lot more then we initially allowed ourselves to be bent.

If we don't deal with our problems, our problems will break us. They will cause us to snap.

Take a few seconds to think about how you can mend a broken elastic band back.
Fixing a broken elastic band is not impossible, but it is incredibly hard.

Is it not better to deal with the pressure before the elastic band reaches snapping point?
Is it not better to lift the weight off the elastic band while it can still handle all the pressure, without additional pressure holding it down?

Think of moments when you just snapped for no reason. You felt angry and irritated with the world and thereafter you felt guilty for going off at someone. This is because all the problems in your life have become so overwhelming that it has caused you to snap.

Dealing with your problems now is not only beneficial for you, but for those around you as well.

...

We're done with section 1.
Well done! You've made a lot of progress. You may find yourself tired from all the thinking, but that's normal.

A quick brief recap of the section:

In this section we gave thought to where we fit in the grand scheme of life. We explored our capabilities, as well as our limitations. We also started becoming cognisant of the abilities and limitations of other people in our life.

We learned how powerful the art of acceptance is and how to view acceptance from a positive angle.

We found that asking for help is not a sign of weakness, but one of the best tools we have on our journey towards emotional freedom.

We saw that, even in negativity, there is positivity. Our negative moments are crucial for us to value and appreciate the positive we will be faced with.

We became willing to assess where we use our *character defects* as a means of manipulation.

We focused on why our traumatic experiences need to be dealt with and the importance of dealing with problems as they arrive.

The following section is perhaps my favourite section of the book. In the following few chapters, we will look at one of the greatest side effects of leaving problems undealt with.

Making Progress

PART TWO – ADDICTION, KILLER OF THE 21ST CENTURY

CHAPTER NINE

Introduction to Addiction

Addiction - killer of the 21st century.

You know I mean business if I have an entire part of the book dedicated to the disease of addiction.

The disease of addiction is a very broad subject, one that would take a whole series of books to go through, so I'm going to go into detailed specifics on every drug or addictive behavior, but still keep the information in this part of the book: to the point, easy to relate to, and specific.

Now I know that many of you may be reading this and thinking, *er...I'm not an addict, why would I even WANT to read this?*

I wrote this book with the aim of helping people find emotional freedom and to help people deal with life's difficult problems.

I therefore felt that it was necessary to include a part dedicated to addiction. We will not be going into depth on the topic in this book, but rather focus on the basics. Using these basic tools we will learn, you will be able to see just how far-spread the disease of addiction is. Use this information to gain a better understanding of the illness, realize how it affects our lives, and what we can do to work around these issues.

More importantly, we will be going through some of the methods people use when trying to numb themselves or deflect from their emotional problems. With more and more people turning to addictive substances or behaviors, I feel it is crucial for me to include this section.

This may be something you're currently suffering with.
Perhaps you fear that if you do not look deep within yourself, you may soon develop the disease of addiction.
Some of you may know of people that you suspect may be an addict.

Perhaps many of you have tried to help either yourselves or a loved one, but you feel that all your efforts were in vain.
Is this because of a lack of trying?
Not always.

It's hard helping someone if you don't know or understand what they're going through.
If your understanding on addiction is like most people's: limited, then this part of the book can prove incredibly helpful to you and/or the person you're trying to help.

In this part of the book I want to show you just how broad the disease of addiction is. To do so, I have focused on the most popular behavioral addictions and not what people typically associate the word with: *severe alcoholics and drug addicts.*
As you read on, you will discover that it really doesn't matter whether I focus on alcohol, drugs, gambling or sex. The symptoms of the addict and the basic concept of addiction remains the same across all addictions.

The disease of addiction is one of the biggest contributors towards people not feeling happy. I therefore encourage you to read through the next few chapters with the hopes that you don't only gain understanding, but know how to apply it all in a practical sense.

CHAPTER TEN

What is addiction?

The first step in dealing with addiction is gaining an understanding on the subject.

Addiction is a very broad subject and I will be releasing more books in the future that look at the different types of addiction in depth - understanding addiction as well as how to work through it. For now, we're just going to focus on the basics.

Many people have negative views of an addict. The reason for this is because many people do not understand the disease of addiction.

As a recovering addict, I write from first-hand experience and try to make things as simple as possible, and easy to read and understand.

My mom, my aunts and those closest to me have tried countless times to help me. When I didn't willingly accept the help, they saw this behavior as a slap in the face - an ungrateful decline of a helping hand.

Of course, back then, I didn't even know or understand what addiction really meant, let alone know what would be beneficial for me. It was only once I learned about the disease of addiction and compared this to my own experiences did all my behaviors, defense mechanisms, and negative coping tools make sense.

I have heard many concepts and to be honest, some of it made sense, but it still left a lot of unanswered questions.

Addiction is not a simple concept to understand. Now if an addict himself doesn't understand the disease, what's the chances of those around the addict getting it?

When I first entered recovery, I was told that, "Addiction is a chronic disease - one that you never recover from." This made no sense to me.
I was told this by one of my counsellors in my first treatment centre.
All I kept thinking was, *If I can't ever recover from this illness, then what the hell am I even doing here?*
I was then told about management programs, again…*what the hell are you on about?*

After many years of struggling with my addiction, it finally all made sense to me. I hope that I can relay my message as clear as possible for you to also have this understanding.

So, what is addiction?
Very simply, when someone is an addict, they have a physical or psychological dependence on either a substance or behavior.
An addict can be addicted to a substance such as prescription pills, cocaine, food, or alcohol. They can also be addicted to a behavior such as sex, shopping, or work.
When the addict uses this substance or behaviour, they get a temporary *high* that allows them to escape reality, even if it's just for a while. This *short lived high,* provides them with the release needed to escape all their problems and they can pretend as if they don't exist.

Addiction is a chronic disease, much like high blood pressure or diabetes. You can live a perfectly normal life, but like diabetes and high blood pressure, it requires daily treatment.
In essence, the people that have gone on to become addicted to either a substance or a particular behavior generally cannot be "cured."
Constant psychological treatment is required and on a daily basis; programs such as AA are very effective because of the constant psychological reassessment required in the program. Addiction is also a cunning disease of the mind. So even though you may feel that they are addicted in one way or another, the addict's mind convinces them otherwise.

Given the above explanation, let's break it down further to gain a deeper understanding of addiction.
You may or may not have heard people refer to the <u>disease of addiction as a chronic disease.</u>

Think about it, how many alcohol "management" plans have you heard about, that work?

By "management," I mean those books that advertise, "Learn How to Control Your Drinking," or "How to Party in Moderation." A major problem I have with these methods is that they do not encourage you to unravel the root cause of the addiction or the emotional turmoil that lies beneath.

Addicts have no concept of moderation. Someone becomes addicted because they use their drug of choice or behavioral addiction obsessively and compulsively.
The most successful addiction management plans include those where you have to completely put down the drug or stop the behavior.

Why do I say that the only solution is complete abstinence?
As a recovery addict, I'm surrounded by people in recovery.
Let me let you in on a little secret on all recovery addicts. *If we could use successfully and in moderation, we would.* But, we can't. We have tried to limit our use, we have tried countless things to use successfully and none of them worked. We only found true sobriety once we made complete life changes and abstained from our substance or behavior.

Now knowing that the only solution for dealing with addiction is complete abstinence, the question is, how does an addict completely abstain from their addiction?

Let's use a few examples to gain a deeper understanding of the troubles an addict is faced with when trying to completely abstain from their addiction.

Let's use a common addiction problem and one that many can relate to - the alcoholic.

The alcoholic will always be faced with alcohol.
At bars, restaurants, supermarkets; they're even faced with alcohol at their favorite sport events.
Okay, so I've mentioned a few of the more obvious places, but what about those that aren't as obvious, such as energy drinks or cough syrup with alcohol.
Since the only way to recover is by means of complete abstinence, surely, he can't have that cough syrup?

Is it possible for them to stay away from all these places and completely avoid all places that sell alcohol?
Should he also avoid all pharmacies that sell cough syrup mixed with alcohol?
Must he never go to a restaurant that cooks food with wine again?

I suppose it is possible, but there's only so much hiding that one can do.

Eventually, they will have to go out into public and they will be faced with temptation. The problem here does not lie with the store's liquor license. The problem lies with the addict.

What's required of the addict?
Not to keep running away from all these places, but rather to start addressing all the underlying issues behind his addiction.
Even with addiction, we need to dig deep in order to recover.

CHAPTER ELEVEN

Signs of an addict

What are the signs of an addict?

You might be reading this section of the book, thinking to yourself, *Why does this even interest me? I highly doubt I'm an addict.*

When most people think of addiction, they picture that homeless guy sitting on the street. He's generally found begging for money and in his spare time, shoots heaps of heroin up his arm.
Surely, that does NOT apply to me. Yeah, I might like my wine, but I haven't gone that far.

If you are one of those people, then I have a very sad, but true reality check for you.
Addiction does not discriminate.
The disease of addiction can affect anyone, some people cover it well and others have hit their rock bottom so hard that it may seem like they can never get back up again.

Regardless of whether you're suffering from the disease of addiction, one of the two options below probably applies to you:

- You fear that you may a have a substance abuse problem or a behavioral addiction.

- You suspect that someone close to you may have a problem. You are just not sure what signs to look out for?

Making Progress

You may have noticed a sudden change in behavior.
You think this person, or yourself, is heading on a downward spiral, but you are just not sure?

Perhaps you want to help them, but your knowledge on addiction is so limited that it makes it even harder for you to help the addict in distress.

For the sake of this chapter, I have used the word, "drug." This refers to all addictive substances, such as weed or alcohol and includes all behavioral addictions.
I have summarized the "warning signs" below and this includes signs of substance abuse and behavioral addictions (sex, gambling, or even addiction to gaming). This a personalized list I can most relate to. There are loads of more signs, but these are the ones that really stand out.

Here's a few tell-tale signs that someone close to you may be suffering from the disease of addiction:

1. Withdrawal from close family and friends
2. Irregular sleeping patterns
3. Lack of appetite
4. Unstable moods
5. Change in behavior and mannerisms
6. Physical signs

Each category is broken down for you to best understand why the addict behaves in such a way and more importantly, whether or not the person may be an addict or not.

Withdrawn from family and friends

Someone that was once an integral part of the family suddenly becomes very quiet and disengaged.

Communication with this person becomes increasing difficult. They almost seem to shut off both physically and emotionally. They may once have reached out for help but no longer see the value in asking for help.

Withdrawal takes two forms:

- Emotional withdrawal

and,

- Physical withdrawal

Emotional withdrawal

All drugs, including alcohol (newsflash, it's a drug) acts as a brain depressant. This leads the potential addict to feel a number of things like depression and fear. The most overwhelming of all, is the anxiety that comes with abuse of substances.
The shame. The guilt. It's all just too much.

Anxiety is caused by constant worry.

Oh my God, will people find out about my addiction?
If they do, what will they think of me?
What if law enforcement finally catches up with me?
Wait! It's a PLANT and it's totally natural, why do I even feel guilty?
Where will I go then?
What will I do?
"Who's there?"   *"Is someone watching me right now?"*

Most importantly, the anxiety kicks in when one has become dependent on the drug and has to find a way to cope without it. This is known as withdrawal symptoms.
The brain believes that the only way to feel normal, is by having the drug again.

Emotional withdrawal is the cause. Physical withdrawal is the result.

Physical withdrawal

The addict becomes very quiet and to the point; only engaging when they absolutely have to and only when it's difficult for them to withdraw. They feel uncomfortable in the company of loved ones and fear they may be asked uncomfortable or confrontational questions about their recent behavior.
They struggle to reach out for help. This sounds like a whole lot of FEAR to me.

Where does that fear stem from?
Fear of reaching out and asking for help is often associated with the shame and guilt associated with the use of addictive substances or destructive behaviors.

   "What will people think of me?"

   "How will they react if or when they find out?"

As a result of this withdrawal, they feel alone and as time goes by and the addiction strengthens, you will find that emotionally numbing themselves becomes a defense mechanism.
The best way to defend themselves is to physically withdraw from the company of others.

The addict may feel like they already have incredibly high standards to live up to and start to feel like failures. Moms and dads that set unachievable, high standards for their kids - this one is for you. The very thing you may be thinking will encourage and drive your son or daughter, might be pushing them away.

Shame and guilt is the main reason people physically withdraw themselves from the company of others.

Sometimes the best way for an addict to withdraw, not only from others, but from themselves as well, is to sleep. This leads us to the second point:

Irregular sleeping patterns

The most obvious sign to look out for, is when the potential addict has difficulty sleeping at night and is constantly in a state of 'being drained' during the day. They may find it hard to focus or concentrate during the day.

On the flip side, the potential addict may just want to sleep all day and night. This is common with dual diagnosed addicts (the addict suffering from addiction and a mental illness, such as depression).

Sleep helps us live longer. Sleep can help bring out our creative bones. It can help with our memory, making everyday tasks like working, studying, and fulfilling our responsibilities easier.

Getting sufficient and quality sleep helps us function normally and with a clear head. <u>Lack of sleep will do the opposite.</u>

Addiction can affect sleep in the following way:

- People with stimulant based addictions struggle to reach the state of calm required because of the increased heart rate or they cannot stop their over active brains from thinking.

- Some people use their addiction as an aid to help them sleep.

<u>Stimulant based sleep disorder</u>

Okay, so firstly, stimulant based sleep disorder is not actually a thing.
I just think it sounds cool, so let's make it a thing.

Here's a little interesting side note: Something I found to be common amongst addicts, especially in early recovery, is their ability to drink coffee and still sleep at night. When I say drink coffee, I mean heaps of it!

Hold up, why am I even mentioning this?

For most people, a cup of coffee is all they need to get their day started. Most people also avoid coffee after 6pm because they will struggle to sleep at night. A lot of the addicts I know, use substances with a lethal and unnatural amount of stimulation. As their body becomes dependent on these stimulants, coffee just doesn't cut it anymore. Why I made mention of this, is to give you an idea of just how stimulated addicts can be. This also gives an easy to understand and practical example of how chemical dependence works.

Stimulants affect the central nervous system.
They cause the addict to be alert and aware.
Their heart beat rate goes through the roof.
They cannot sleep and when they do, the sleep is of very poor quality. Poor quality sleep leaves them feeling tired the following day.

<u>People that use their addiction as an aid to help them sleep.</u>

Some addicts, cannot handle the effects of not having proper sleep. These addicts cross addict to other drugs in an attempt to help them sleep "better."
Ever heard of *cross addiction?* This is an example of how cross addiction can occur.

Other people are addicted to substances that help them sleep, such as sleeping pills. This normally starts when someone is faced with overwhelming stress, anxiety, or depression. They use these substances to reach a state of normality. Their dependence on these drugs increases and when they try to quit, it's a nightmare to sleep.

<u>Lack of exercise.</u>
Another important aspect to take into account is that a lot of addicts don't exercise regularly. Those that do exercise either do it excessively or aren't really gaining value from the exercise as the substances counteract any benefits they would have gained from exercise. Exercise has been proven to help people have a better night's rest. For many people, daily exercise is essential to a good night's rest.

Change in behaviors:

The addict may have had a lot of interests that would previously occupy their free time and this included positive recreational interests that made them happy. The addict may also start neglecting responsibilities that were once important to them.

"Oh my god, SHUT UP! I don't care! It's my life, damnit!"

Many addicts develop an "I don't care attitude."
It's quite obvious what the problem is, right?
Arrogance!...Hmmm, not quite.
Let's take a moment to understand where the, "I don't care attitude," comes from.
This is a defense mechanism. Arrogance is often an unfounded defense mechanism.

People generally cannot stand a narcissist with an attitude of grandeur. Everyone tends to keep their distance from such people.
It's quite common for many addicts to have this attitude. Why do a lot of addicts have this attitude though? The short answer is to keep people at a distance.
Keeping people at bay makes it much more manageable to continue with their addiction without any interference.
Makes sense?
By pretending to be an asshole, the addict chases people away and can continue with his or her addiction. Addicts aren't actually assholes, it's really just a mask worn to protect our addiction.

As our values change, so does the circle of friends we keep. People stick together.
That's the reason why you find so many online niche forums or why people have preferences of what they look for in a potential partner.
People hang around people that share similar interests.
Another noticeable change in behavior would be a sudden change in the company the potential addict keeps.
These are big warning signs. They may have neglected their "good" friends and replaced them with new ones.

One of the biggest tell-tale signs is that of stealing, lying, and an overall inconsistency of stories.

Again, these are all coping mechanisms the addict becomes accustomed to, and they are used purely for survival.
When an addict lies, they do not always lie because they simply enjoy lying. They do so to protect their addiction.

Making Progress

Att: non-addicts:

Picture yourself being deprived of food…Right now, your brain tells you that you need food in order to survive, right? Now imagine if someone were to take away your food for a week. Would you either: be content with the idea of starving to death or would you do anything in your power to defend the little food you have left.

The same logic applies with addicts. They are chemically or psychologically dependent on their drug or habit of choice.

The message their brain sends the rest of their body is that they cannot survive without the substance or the addictive behavior. Naturally, they develop negative defense mechanisms to defend the one thing their brain tells them they need the most.

That is why addicts lie, cheat, steal, and even become aggressive.

Unstable moods

The potential addict may be extremely happy one minute and in the next, a complete shift in mood. They then become a nightmare to be around. Some drugs may even cause you to hallucinate causing the addict to live in a state of constant fear.

Emotional extremes.

As humans, we are only equipped to deal with a certain amount of happiness or sadness. Think back to the elastic band theory.
Because the addict is so dependent on substances or their behavior to reach a state of normality, when the addict withdraws from their drug, they feel overwhelming anxiety. Most people do not know how to deal with this and as a result, their mind and body enters a state of shock, this is what causes the complete change in moods.

Many drugs, especially stimulants like cocaine, provide insane and unnatural feelings of euphoria.

That being said, what goes up must come down, right?

When the suffering addict comes down, he would then feel the exact opposite of what he initially felt. Extreme happiness turns into deep and dark depression,

even grief.
That is, not to mention all the other side effects that comes with it.

The human brain is not designed to handle these extreme highs or lows.

Physical signs

Something that is very important to take into account is that:

As the addiction progresses, the addict's self-esteem regresses.

As the addict sinks deeper into the grips of addiction, little else matters.

The reason for that is twofold:
1) They start feeling unworthy of love, of affection.
2) They develop an overall lack of self-love. Again, this is associated with the shame and guilt that comes with addiction.

I cannot stress how important this is in order to understand an addict in distress.

Because of the high the addict gets out of the behavior or substance; the addict becomes physically and psychologically dependent. Their mind and body craves that fix, so focusing on their physical wellbeing becomes much harder to do.

Finally, what are the physical signs or symptoms of addiction? This may be the easiest of the tell-tale signs, because it becomes harder for the addict to maintain the illusion of "being fine" as the disease of addiction progresses.

Addicts lose interest in their overall wellbeing. There are many tell-tale signs, but I have highlighted a few of which I think are very important and could mean that *urgent* help is required.

<u>Blood shot eyes</u>

They constantly appear on edge. Those once sparkly, white eyes start becoming redder than the blood river itself. They may even add two tubes of eye gene on the monthly shopping list to try and hide this. Their pupils could also be dilated. The reason the addict's pupils are dilated is because the brain is in a state of shock with the adrenaline pump to the brain.

<u>Unfavorable odours</u>

After becoming dependent on their drug, the addict needs their fix to reach a state of normality.

Spending time on personal hygiene becomes very difficult and they start neglecting this. They forget or are too preoccupied to brush their teeth, they may start wearing the same clothes, or only bathing once a week.

As mentioned, the depressant effects become stronger and an overall lack of self-love becomes more and more evident.

Appetite

Addiction affects people in different ways. The one that is always constant though, is a change in appetite.

Some addicts experience a complete lack of appetite and go for days without food. They become dizzy, may have short panic attacks, constant anxiety, and an overall feeling of weakness. This is because the addict is not consuming sufficient nutrients to sustain their body.

On the flip side, some addicts may have an increased craving for junk food. A lot of addicts resort to junk food especially when craving their substance of choice. The sugar provides them with rush of happy endorphins, much like drugs.

The change in appetite is largely dependent on the substance or behaviour they're addicted to.

Irregular heartbeat

Some drugs can cause a reduced heartbeat and others may increase it to a deathly rate. The addict may suffer from a shortness of breath because of all the pressure placed on the heart.

Chest pains become the norm. They could start sweating uncontrollably. Panic attacks could follow. I have experienced all of these conditions and it is truly a terrible place to be in. My health deteriorated to the point that I no longer felt the will to live.

Unexplainable marks on body

This is especially common with addicts that use needles. There are usually unexplainable marks on their arms. Other marks on the body include: scars, black bags under the eyes due to the lack of sleep, and a change in skin color. The addict's appearance suddenly becomes dull and pale. Their lips may become very dark as well.

I have read many articles on the web describing and listing the warning signs of addiction. A lot of articles list what to look out for, but few give an in-depth

understanding of why the addict behaves in such a manner.
What are the driving factors for these behaviors?

Understanding why the addict behaves in a certain way is one of the biggest steps you can take towards helping the addict.

What is **_SO IMPORTANT_** is that you begin to shift your focus from, *What must I look out for?* to, *why does he, she or myself behave in this manner?*

The addict in distress does not need your sympathy, in fact, it may just cause more harm.
If you really want to help the addict, empathize with them by understanding why they do what they do.
I have tried to place a lot of emphasis on understanding the psychological and physical side of all of these warning signs.

Now that we have a decent understanding of addiction, many people might want to either start dealing with their own addiction or helping someone they suspect may be an addict.

Easy tiger! Just because you have a better understanding of an addict doesn't necessarily mean they want whatever help you have on offer.

The next chapter focuses on how to deal with addicts that do not want the help.

CHAPTER TWELVE

Helping an addict that does not want help

Before you read on, I need to make another important note.

Attention, all non-addicts:

When life starts spiralling out of control, the addict is not blinded to the negative effects the addiction has on his or her life. A big misconception that many people have is that addicts simply don't give a shit. This is not the case. Most addicts try helping themselves, but like you, they don't know how.

Everyone has come across an addict that they felt needed help. Whether this person had a direct relation with them or not.
We would get upset after having tried everything to help the addict, only for our efforts to be thrown in our face.

At one stage or another, we have probably come across that one person that's very dear to us that struggles with the disease of addiction. They are that one person we have decided deserves a fighting chance.
That person may be a very close friend, a family member, or a co-worker. That person may even be yourself.

For a while, we've been observing their every move. After reading the previous chapter, we may even be completely convinced they suffer from the dreaded disease of addiction.
It first started when you noticed a sudden change in behavior. Things that were

once important to them, are now being neglected. They may have been very family orientated, but suddenly became very distant. Often ignoring calls from family members, declining invitations to family gatherings. New excuses, different days.
Items may suddenly start disappearing and they would get incredibly defensive when you ask them about it. There's a certain inconsistency in their behaviour. Their stories just do not add up anymore and any trust you once had in them is gone.

Once their change in behavior becomes more and more obvious, they become defensive and blame their behavior on everything and everyone else. Clearly holding onto deep and dark anger, they continue down this path. You may even have heard stories from other people convinced that they may have a problem. Hell, you may not even need to have heard those stories. You might even have caught them gambling obsessively or drinking more than they should.

What's the most natural thing to do?
You try everything in your power to help the addict.
You read this book with the greatest concentration because there's nothing that you want more than to help.

Again, it's important to note that the addict I'm referring to could be someone close to you or yourself (if you suspect *you* may have an addiction problem).

Sudden emergency family interventions are organized to discuss how to help. We try talking to the addict; we tell them that we suspect they may have a problem and offer them whatever help we can think of.
Some people go as far as begging to help. Worried moms and dads even try phoning the police in hopes that they would get locked up and learn their lesson.

Parents can be found in tears, often casting blame on themselves for the course their child's life has taken.
"Where did I go wrong?"
"If only I been a better mother, this would never have happened!"

The point that I'm trying to make is that you are now equipped with every reason to believe this person needs help.

After trying everything in your power to help the addict, you eventually give up. You then think that all your attempts were in vain and we start developing a strong dislike and anger towards the addict.
As this anger strengthens over time, you may find the addict to be very ungrateful and undeserving of love. After all your attempts to help, it was simply thrown in your face.

Here's the problem: YOU ARE CONVINCED THAT THEY ARE AN ADDICT. THEY ARE NOT.

Let's go back to the initial definition.

Addiction is seen as a chronic disease, much like high-blood pressure or diabetes. You can live a perfectly normal life, but it would require daily treatment.

Given the above, let's break it down further to gain an even deeper understanding of addiction.
The only solution for dealing with addiction is complete abstinence.

Here's the thing though: the addict cannot work on treatment until they actually realize they have a problem that needs to be worked on. If the addict doesn't acknowledge that they have a problem, they won't fix the problem.

Personally, I refused to believe that I was an addict for many years.
I often thought it was simply a phase I was going through and that I was just "having fun."
As my life progressively spiralled out of control, denying my addiction became harder to do. Even then, when someone merely suggested that I could be an addict, I would become very defensive, angered by the thought of them even suggesting I was an addict.
I would find so many justifications; convincing myself that I did not need help. This is the process that many addicts in recovery have gone through. In fact, it's completely normal. Who wants to identify themselves as an addict? It's certainly not something to brag about, right?

The reality is that unless that addict realizes that he or she may have a problem, there is very little that can be done. It's sad, but true.

Constantly trying to help the addict may not be the best solution for them. In fact, you might even be doing more harm than good by enabling them. Their behaviour may never change, because they know that someone will catch them every time they fall.

The addict in distress needs empathy, not sympathy.

Sometimes, the only way we can love an addict is to let them fall.

The last few chapters have been dedicated towards developing a decent understanding of the disease of addiction. A disease that so many turn to; to try and cover their problems.

The next three chapters will be spent to see how universal the disease of addiction is. In these chapters, I've focused on three of the most common behavioural addictions.

I focused on these behavioural addictions to show how addiction reveals itself in many ways and is not limited to alcohol or drugs.

CHAPTER THIRTEEN
Dealing with an eating addiction

You wake up in the middle of the night searching for anything to eat. You become grumpy and irritable if you haven't had chocolate in a while.

You look at the scale and become more depressed because that number just keeps growing. This is depressing, so for you to feel better, you eat more. It becomes a horrible ongoing cycle and you know it will only get worse, but you can't stop.

Many people wonder if they have a problem with food.
Food addiction is a serious problem and one of the main reasons that some people can't control themselves around bad food, no matter how hard they try.

What is an eating addiction?

Very simply, food addiction is being addicted to junk food, much like the drug addict is addicted to cocaine.

To understand food addiction, you need a basic level of understanding addiction.

Addiction, is the excessive or compulsive use of a substance or behavior, despite knowing there are severe and serious consequences.

It's the inability to stop, despite all attempts to moderate the use of bad foods or cut down.
Similar to addictive drugs, foods high in carbs and sugars release feel-good triggers in the brain.

That is exactly what food addiction is: eating large amounts of unhealthy foods, whilst well knowing it only causes more harm than good.

The person with an overeating addiction develops an unhealthy relationship with food. Food addiction is a behavioral addiction that much like gambling, sex, or shopping, triggers intense temporary pleasure.

When a cocaine addict uses cocaine, a great amount of dopamine gets released in the brain. These neurotransmitters are the reward centres or the feel-good creators in the brain. The human body is designed to handle only so much though, it is not designed to handle insane highs or lows (think depression).

When a food addict eats foods that are highly processed and high in sugars, fats, or even salt, these feel-good transmitters (dopamine) are released. That is why eating junk food is so pleasurable.

These reward signals override feelings of fullness and that is why people addicted to food keep eating, even after knowing they have had way too much.

In essence, the food addict, much like the cocaine addict, chases a constant high.

The problem: the more they eat, the more their tolerance for food increases.

The more this person eats, the more dopamine gets released. Dopamine is the brain's reward centre. They give us those good feelings and we get happy. As human beings, we are only designed to handle so much dopamine though.

I want you to think of it this way:
Try understanding why we feel happy.
What makes us happy?
How do we know that; *okay, right now I'm soo happy, I'm slightly short of daisies coming out my ass?*
Recognizing happiness is a result of us being able to recognize sadness. Without sadness, we would be in a constant state of "happiness." But then this feeling is no longer a "reward." This state of happiness becomes your norm, almost what you expect from life.

That's how addiction works on a psychological level. As the food addict's tolerance for food increases, he or she needs this release of dopamine to reach a state or feeling of normality. Less dopamine gets released with each *relapse*, but they need more, and the only way they can get more is by increasing their food intake or portion sizes. That is how addiction works, regardless of the substance.

As the disease of addiction thickens; they feel worse about themselves. They try rationing their foods, they go on diets, controlled eating plans, they try that whole "eating in moderation" thing. All of this with little success. They feel miserable when they have not had their fix. They are grumpy, agitated, and discontent and the only way they can remove these feelings and hopefully feel better about themselves, is to have more food.

Here's a scary thought for you to digest: drug addicts and alcoholics receive more compassion and empathy than those with chronic addictions to food. Drug addicts and alcoholics don't get a lot of sympathy from others. This just tells you how much more the food addict is faced with hatred and judgment.

Contrary to what many people may think, being addicted to food is not due to greediness or a lack of will power. Such thinking is just ignorant. Yes, people addicted to food may have made bad choices with food, but thinking of such a person as lazy, weak, or greedy is naive. The person has become dependent on food and that is why they struggle to stop. Their brain believes they can only survive by having junk food. Rewiring their brain is very difficult, and that is the process of recovery.

Before we go on, let's squash another myth.

While obesity could be a sign indicating that someone may suffer with an overeating addiction, it does not make it a clear sign that someone is addicted to food. That is, that they have an emotional or physical dependence on food.

Signs or symptoms of food addiction

Unlike drugs or alcohol, detecting food addiction is not as simple. There are no blood or urine tests for food addiction. You may have frequent tests that reflect high cholesterol levels, high blood pressure, you may even have developed diabetes. None of these tests are sure ways to detect if you or someone you love suffers from the disease of addiction.

What makes detection even harder is when the person is completely unwilling to be honest about his or her eating habits.

How would you know if you may suffer from an eating addiction?

The first and most important tool in identifying any possible issues with an overeating addiction, is complete honesty. The same honesty that is required for all other addictions.

While there may be no obvious tests to determine if someone has a problem, there are a few signs and symptoms to look out for.

Ask yourself the below questions to find out if you may have a problem:

    1) Do you hide the amount of food you eat from others?

2) Do you try quitting junk food, only to find that a few days, sometimes hours later, you give in to your cravings and end up eating even more than you should have?

3) Have you tried countless diets designed to control your eating, but none of them seem to last?

4) Are you super creative with some of the excuses you come up with for why you should eat?

5) Do you have feelings of guilt and shame when eating certain foods?

6) Do you have constant cravings, even when you're full?

7) You realize the physical and emotional effects of over eating unhealthy foods, yet you can't seem to stop yourself from consuming these foods?

If the answers to the questions above leave you feeling uncomfortable, because some of it may ring true, then continue reading.

Effects of an eating disorder

What often begins as an innocent passion for food, turns out to be deadly.

The most visibly obvious of the dangers associated with overeating are the physical side effects. That's the first thing people notice - the sudden weight gain. What people often don't see is just how much deeper the addiction affects the food addict on a mental and psychological level.

Anyone that suffers from an overeating addiction, leads a perilous life with no real sense of happiness anymore.

To illustrate this, let's discuss some of the dangers involved when you consume junk food excessively. The three main areas affected in the food addict's life is their physical, mental and social wellbeing.

Physical side effects

Most of the physical side effects suffered are health related. People that eat junk food excessively are more likely to suffer from diabetes, high cholesterol, or kidney disease amongst many other physical illnesses. The more they eat, the more overweight they become, leading to bone deterioration and arthritis. Having too much fatty tissue in our bodies, can be a direct result in a lot of functions failing such as the heart, kidney, and lungs.

A food addict's immune system weakens as they are most likely not receiving enough vitamins and nutrients. With the added stress of increasing medical bills, maintaining a healthy physical image becomes almost impossible.

Mental side effects

As with most illnesses, there is a great deal of emotional turmoil that occurs. Sometimes the emotional side effects kick in before the physical side effects even begin to surface.

Think back to a time when you ate excessively, only to get on the scale and realize that the damned number just keeps going higher, or that none of your clothes fit anymore.
You need to buy new clothes, which is a great idea, but you don't have the money to do so.
You look in the mirror and try your hardest to hide that double chin you're fast gaining.
What's the first emotion that hits you with a wave of vengeance? Depression.
Look at me, I'm disgusting!
How could I have let myself go like this?

As the weight gain increases and all physical side effects kick in, the overeater feels and thinks poorly of him or herself.

The distressed addict loses any confidence they once had. They no longer feel deserving of other people's company, or even of their own company. As a result, they eat more in a desperate attempt to escape their harsh reality.
The emotional component that comes with the disease of addiction is the biggest reason a person struggles to stop.

There is a complete lack of control once they eat again and this leaves the addict feeling weak or that they lack any willpower to control their eating. Their self-esteem plummets. Constantly hiding food consumption raises anxiety, the addict becomes a nervous wreck. To top things off, they face constant feelings of shame and guilt and so the process of self-hatred begins.

It's clear that the emotional side effects of a chronic overeater can be severe, but if you think that's bad, the negative side effects continue.

Social side effects

As the emotional side effects kick in and the overeater enters a state of depression and all other mental illnesses that come with having a low self-esteem, their social life takes a huge backseat. Once an addict starts isolating from the rest of the world, the knock-on effect is that this leaves them with even deeper loneliness and depression.

Because of the poor nutrition the overeater receives, the overeater is more susceptible to sleeping disorders. As we have already discussed, sleep is essential for our wellbeing and for us to function normally. In a very short period of time, the addict develops an overall poor quality of life.

The shame and guilt leads them to social isolation. This does not just end with his or her social circles or friends, but this goes as far as their family life and even their career.

Rewarding ourselves with food is completely normal, so is overeating occasionally, but when food, more especially, junk food, becomes our crutch, the side effects can be severe.

A lot more severe than we might have initially given it thought.

How to deal with an eating disorder

The overeater consumes a large amount of processed or junk food, because it provides them with a temporary release from psychological stress. It also provides a diversion from the weighing feelings of shame and guilt.

I specially chose to include this as one of the behavioral addictions in this book because this is one of the most widespread addictions.
This is also something I struggled with personally and my food consumption is still something that weighs heavily on my mind. Nowadays, as soon as I find myself over-eating, I stop and determine what void I'm trying to fill or if there is a lack in any of the other areas of my life.
This could include financial stress, loneliness, or anger. I've identified these as the main areas of concern.

Everyone else would have different reasons for over-eating and if you are an over-eater, it's up to you to identify what your trigger emotions are.
I did a lot of research and started attending over-eaters anonymous meetings.

This helped me gain a lot of insight on addiction and it was at this point that I realized my overeating addiction is exactly like my drug, alcohol, gambling, and sex addiction.
The insight I gained taught me that the disease of addiction is not limited to one behavior or drug.

Addiction manifests itself in many ways and that is how you find that a lot of recovering alcoholics turn to food, once they put the bottle down.

Dealing with an overeating addiction is difficult. It's as difficult, if not, more difficult than a heroin addict giving up the needle.

The negative image people have on those that have an overeating addiction makes matters worse, it makes reaching out and asking for help that much harder. We fear being viewed as weak, lazy, or greedy.

What makes treating an overeating addiction a nightmare, is that food is not something we can escape. For us to survive and for our bodies to sustain itself, we have to eat.

Unhealthy food is easily accessible, everywhere you turn you will find a fast food joint. You may have a healthy grocery shopping list, but you still cannot avoid the chocolates and other processed food items as you wait in the queue in your local supermarket.
These bad foods are not something we can escape. That is a reality we must face and accept.

Another reality that we have to accept is that the food is not the problem.
WE are the problem.

The real work comes in when you have to train your body and mind to neglect the bad, unhealthy food we have come to rely on. These *bad* foods will need to be replaced with healthier foods that sustain us and provide our bodies with the nutrition it requires.

Withdrawal symptoms

If you are addicted to food, you will know whenever you try quitting the unhealthy processed and junk foods. You'll experience withdrawal symptoms. The same withdrawals that an alcoholic has after a few days of not having a drink.

Withdrawal symptoms include: irritation, snappiness with others, unexplainable mood swings, feelings of worthlessness, and immense sadness.

We experience these withdrawal symptoms because our body has become so used to having these substances that when these substances are taken away from us, we do not know how to cope with life.
They have become our only coping mechanism.

The solution?

Before we delve into any suggested routes of recovery, let's remember the golden rule and that is:

> *For addiction, moderation fails. Every time.*

Another important thing to mention is that this chapter is only written for those who truly believe they have a problem with eating.
If you do not fully believe you have an eating disorder or are willing to accept that the foods you eat are doing more harm than good, then these tools are not for you.
If you find yourself faced with other problematic areas of addiction, then this chapter applies to you. We have seen how easy it is to cross addict to other substances, especially when our underlying issues aren't dealt with.

Recovery begins with accepting and then deciding to never eat these bad foods again.
It's as simple as that.
We have to accept our problem and then *want* to quit, without any reservations. We accept it, not because we are weak, but because we are fighting for the quality of life we know we deserve.

While there are many ways to treat an overeating addiction, the best solution, is complete abstinence.

Unlike other addictions, completely abstaining from junk food can be very hard, but making that decision to *not want* to eat these foods goes a long way dealing with the addiction.

Like drug addicts or alcoholics, the only way to recover is by completely cutting off these bad foods.
The addict addicted to junk food cannot eat in moderation. This has been proven time and time again. They wish they could eat these foods successfully, but they can't.
The Alcoholics anonymous book said this best,
An addict is a person that suffers from the disease of addiction, they have to remain free all of addictive substances to recover.

Relapses

Be prepared for relapses.
The most important thing to remember when embarking on your road towards recovery, is that you did not become addicted to food overnight.

> It is unfair for you to think you will have the *whole recovery from the addiction thing* whacked overnight.

Starting your journey of recovery will be one of the most rewarding tasks of your life. It will also be one of the hardest roads you will ever embark on. The key to recovery, like all good things in life, is not to give up.
If you keep working on your triggers and the underlying reasons behind your addiction, you will eventually get it right.

The good news with over eating is that once you have trained your body to crave healthy foods, having that extra sugar from a bar of chocolate almost seems like a shock to your system. As your become stronger, you will crave the nutrients provided from the healthier foods you eat.

Suggested routes for recovery

12 step programs

Overeater's anonymous is a great fellowship to begin with. They believe that by working through your difficulties with other like-minded people, your chances of recovery are greatly improved. As an overeater, we have isolated ourselves from the outside world, we have so much guilt and shame that we do not know how to discuss this with anyone. Having a helpful support group is one of our greatest assets in recovery.

The approach they take is to not only address the issue at hand, but to address the root cause of the problem.
In this program, you will undress all your fears, your hates, your resentments, and people whom you have harmed with your addiction, and you work through all these areas as your recovery strengthens.

There is a reason why it is one of the most effective tools for gaining freedom from overeating and that is because it's aimed at addressing all underlying issues as well as coming up with a plan to strive towards every day. Be sure to check out their site to locate your nearest meeting. They also have online meetings for those unable to attend physical meetings.

> Check out their site: https://oa.org/

Psychologist or therapy

An overeating addiction is your main problem, but until you deal with the root cause of the problem, the problem will always persist.

Therapy is very helpful in this regard. You get to uncover everything that has been holding you back.
When we eat copious amounts of junk or processed foods, we do so in an attempt to escape our reality. Once you deal with the issues you're running away from, conquering this illness becomes that much easier.

These deep underlying issues need to be addressed for you to find recovery. Food addiction does not just go away or fix itself. Having a professional, trained in helping realize and uncover these issues can be one of the most helpful tools at your disposal.

Bonus tips

We may not be able to avoid fast food restaurants or that chocolate wrapper on the shelf, but there are a few things we can do to make our life easier.

1) Avoid fast food places. In the beginning, it will be very hard to do.
If you often stop at a drive thru after work or on your way to a grocery store, you may want to find alternative routes. This is only until you're strong enough and if the cravings are too intense to handle in the beginning.

2) Try to avoid going on diets – I know this may sound weird, but diets are intended for short term weight loss.
They are designed to be a temporary weight loss solution and is not something sustainable in the long run. The reality is that once the diet is over, people go back to their bad eating habits and are back at square one. The problem with diets are that they can be very tempting. The promise to lose 30 pounds in 3 weeks is enough to lure in even the most hardened food addicts. Recovery is a lifelong journey, it's not something that can be easily achieved over night.

3) Try not to focus on weight loss as your goal. Having weight loss as your primary goal can increase the risk of cross addicting to another addiction, such as bulimia.

This adds on to the second tip. Weight loss is certainly one of the great benefits of starting recovery, but it should never be the main goal. Remember, your goal is to live the life you deserve, free of guilt, shame, and anger. Aim for that and you ensure that you have a solid foundation for your recovery.

4) Ensure that you have your meals planned – because you need to be aware of everything you put in your mouth; having well planned meals is essential.
You should be able to know what's for breakfast on Friday or what's for supper on Sunday. Not having proper meal plans can increase the risk of eating unhealthy, convenient foods.

5) Write a Pro and Con list – In order for you to want recovery, you need to assess that you know why recovery is good for you and why maintaining the current unhealthy life style only works to your detriment.
Draw up a pro and con list for your recovery plan.

6) Identify trigger foods. Many people have that ultimate crutch. Be it ice cream, chocolate, or hamburgers. Identify your trigger foods and ensure that you stay away from these at all cost.

Conclusion

For addiction, moderation fails.

An overeating addiction is the same as someone addicted to drugs or alcohol.

The risks of overeating are far greater than we may have given thought. But, there are ways for us to overcome this illness.

Like all other addictions, complete abstinence is required.

CHAPTER FOUREEN

Dealing with a shopping addiction

"Oh my God! There's a sale! 40% off everything," she shouts.
"Babe, what do you possibly need, that you don't already have?" he barks.
"Oh, you silly man. You can never have too many pairs of shoes!"

Shopping addiction - the glamorous addiction

Shopping is normal, in fact, we need to shop in order to survive.
When your shopping becomes compulsive, that's when it becomes a problem.

What is a shopping addiction?

Very simply, someone that suffers from a shopping addiction spends compulsively. They spend to the point where it affects their life negatively.

It starts off as something normal, even innocent. As the disease progresses, the need to buy more increases.
People with a shopping addiction get a high from making purchases, similar to those that drink or use drugs. The temporary high they get comes from spending and buying things that make them feel better about themselves or it helps them feel better about something they don't want to deal with, such as depression.

The shopaholic spends to the point where their behaviors have adverse effects,

Making Progress

often leading to negative character defects such as stealing or lying to support their habit.
They spend compulsively, regardless of whether they have the financial means to do so or not.

People with a shopping addiction could buy everything they see compulsively or they could be addicted to purchasing a certain product, such as clothing, jewelry, food, playing with the markets, or even real estate.
While research has shown that women are more likely to suffer from this disease, men are fast developing this habit as well. With the increased popularity of metro-sexual males, shopping for men has now become cool - so has the need to look better, dress better, and own better stuff than the next.

Shopping spree VS Shopping addiction

Many people spoil themselves and go on a shopping spree. This is not bad in any way. In fact, it can be positive and have many health benefits.
You get to unwind and buy items of value, or whatever makes you happy with your hard-earned money.
There's a big difference between people that go on shopping sprees and those with a shopping addiction.

Spending excessively in a shopping spree means that you usually have the money and financial means to spend that extra bit of cash.
Shopping sprees are not regular, it's generally a once-in-a-while thing to spoil yourself.
Shopping addicts spend money that they do not necessarily have. They want something and will buy it, even when they don't have the means to do so. Often this means they would get themselves into debt by maxing out their credit cards or taking out loans to support their habits.

Shopaholics go on "shopping sprees" all the time. They do not limit themselves to spend only when they have the excess cash.

Why people develop shopping addictions

Let's face it, nobody is born with a thriving urge to shop. Have you ever wondered why you shop the way you do? Why do you continue buying things you know you can't afford?
There are several reasons that could link to your shopping problems.
You could have been brought up in a home where the value of money was never taught. Perhaps you shop in an attempt to fit in and be cool. You could even use your shopping addiction to cover pain and hurt.

Consumerism
"Calling all shopaholics - 50% sale off everything. One day only."

I did a quick Google search on shopaholics. There are a few articles that may be of great use with treating a shopping addiction, but there are even more articles that glamorize the addiction.

In this day and age, everyone wants to be better than the next, they want more respect than the other person.
The easiest way to stand out from the crowd is by means of material possessions. Think about it, you simply don't view the guy driving the Porsche in the same light as you would the guy driving the 1993 run-down Toyota.
Shopping is one of the biggest means of establishing a social elite.
This also makes shopping addictions more eminent in the wealthier parts of the world where, to put it bluntly, competition if rife.

Social acceptance
Loneliness is one of the biggest contributing factors when it comes shopping excessively. When you walk around a mall with friends or family, shopping till you drop, you all share in on the high.
This provides that much needed sense of belonging.

Emotional issues
Many people don't need a particular item, but they wanted it, so they bought it. Simple as that right?
Wrong.

People shop when they're feeling down. This could be after their heart was broken or they could even suffer with depression. Shopping provides us with that pick-me-up feeling. It gives a temporary release when we're feeling down.

Shopping excessively provides a temporary, numbing relief from pain, much like alcohol and drugs does.

Symptoms of a Shopaholic

There are no tests available to determine whether you have a shopping problem or not.
If you often overspend, not thinking about how you will survive for the rest of the month, there's a big chance that you may have a shopping addiction.

The shopaholic gets the same high from making purchases that the drug addict gets from taking drugs after a long and painful withdrawal.
Many shopaholics portray an image of success and wealth. This is not the case though, they are deep in debt, struggling to pay off loans and credit card bills. They pretend to have money, when in truth, they are broke.
You might only need one new pair of shoes, but end up walking out of the shop with 5.

There's a few questions that you can ask yourself and if any of it rings true, then you might have a problem:

Do you often overspend, even when you don't have the money to do so?
Have you ever lied about your shopping and made it seem less serious than it actually is?
Has your shopping ever brought on feelings of guilt and shame?
Has any of your personal relationships ever suffered because of your shopping?
Do you spend money when you are angry, tired, depressed, or anxious?
Do you get a rush when you shop - an unnatural feeling of happiness?
Have you ever gotten into trouble because of your shopping, but yet you continue to shop?

I'm not going to say, if you answered yes to three or more of these questions, you are a shopaholic.
I'm not trying to sell the idea to you.
If you have a problem with shopping, after having answered these questions, you would know by now.

Effects of a shopping addiction

"Babe, what did you do with your salary? You honestly can't be broke yet?"
"I know! I'm sorry, I didn't mean to spend it all. I really don't know what got into me," she pleads.
"This is why I can't trust you with anything!" With this statement hanging in the air, he storms off.

Shopping provides an immediate emotional release, but the short and long terms effects can be devastating.
Many people buy unnecessary items that remain unused.
There are physical, financial and emotional side effects of an untreated shopping addiction.
All side effects are interrelated. Let's go through each of these side effects.

Making Progress

<u>Financial side effects</u>
This is the most obvious side effect.
Spending money we don't have will result in a vicious debt cycle. Maxed out credit cards become the norm. We open new accounts and apply for new credit cards to pay off our other debt and continue shopping.
Eventually we get to the point where we don't even pay off our debt anymore, resulting in us being blacklisted.

Some people resort to lying and stealing to maintain their lifestyle.

<u>Emotional side effects</u>
Finances play an integral part in our emotional wellbeing. Not being able to pay for transport or rent for the rest of the month is a sure way to leave us feeling worried and anxious.
Add in the feelings of guilt and shame that come with overspending and we are guaranteed a recipe for a breakdown.

As time goes on, shopping is no longer fun. We become anxious because we know that we might not be able to control our spending. Some of us may even isolate to prevent ourselves from spending money we don't have.

Finally, shopping becomes an unhealthy coping mechanism. We use shopping to fill any voids we may have, to cover up any hurt and pain we go through.
Soon this becomes our only coping mechanism.

The one thing that is supposed to make us feel better now makes us feel worse.

<u>Physical side effects</u>
With all the emotional side effects, we suffer the consequences physically. We feel regret or remorse over our spending, but we continue to shop. Our friends and family start disowning us, yet we cannot stop.

The side effects of compulsive spending can be overwhelming, but more often than not, many people only ask for help once they reached their rock bottom and have no other means to hide their addiction any longer.

How to deal with a shopping addiction

Dealing with a shopping addiction is no easy feat - this is one of those "practice makes perfect" cases.

A shopping addiction is very similar to food addictions, it's not something that can just be ignored and pretend it doesn't exist. In order for us to sustain ourselves, we need to eat, we need clothes, and we need basic toiletries. Ceasing to make any further purchases is not a cure for a shopping addiction. If anything, it might actually make things worse.

Like all other addictions, the first step to dealing with the problem is admitting there is a problem. Denial will be the biggest downfall for anyone trying to deal with their addiction. Ultimately, help cannot be forced on anyone with a shopping problem.
The decision to want help or to change lies with that person.

How to avoid a shopping binge
The road to recovery for a shopaholic is a long winded and often painful one. You will be faced with urges to spend money and it will become increasingly difficult as time goes on. Spending excessively has become the norm so putting an end to reckless spending will be very uncomfortable.

Pay for everything with cash – Credit cards can be useful, but they can also be pure evil. By paying for everything with cash, you get to limit yourself to the amount of money you can spend. If you are in a shop and only have 20 bucks, with all your other cards at home, that is all you can spend.

Sure, you might take a drive back home to fetch your cards, but we're hoping that by the time you do that, you're not in the mood to go back and spend more money you don't have.

Shopping list - Know exactly what you need to buy beforehand. Nothing that you buy should be of any surprise to you. Once you know what you need to buy, you will know how much money you need to take with you.

The key to a shopping list is not simply writing down bread and milk.
Your shopping list needs to be as specific as possible. If you need shoes, you need to write down the brand, the type of shoe you need, and the budget allocated for those shoes.
Remember, you have a shopping problem - if you are presented with the opportunity, you will try to manipulate yourself into thinking that you need shoes more expensive or fancier than you actually do.

Get rid of your credit cards - While credit cards can be very useful, if you are trying to curb your spending, credit cards can be your biggest obstacle.
Many people think that by getting rid of their credit cards, the problem would be solved. This might fuel your addiction - everybody wants what they cannot have. This is especially true for the addict.

The last thing you want to tell an addict is,
"No, you may not have this credit card anymore!"
They will make it their mission to get a new card or apply for more debt.
If you are going to keep a credit card, consider handing in the card to someone close to you for emergency purchases. Remember, this solution is not permanent, it is only until you're strong enough and trust yourself enough to curb your spending on your own.

Avoid sales - Those big red banners advertising large discounts are evil.
Refer to your list.
If it's not on your list, you do not need it.

Gifts - a lot of excess spending occurs around holidays or special occasions such as birthdays. Retailers know that majority of people leave their shopping for the last minute and spike up the prices because they have no other option but to buy. Avoid this by planning in advance and buying gifts weeks or even months in advance.

The above points are tools you can use to help prevent unnecessary spending. The solution does not lie in these tools.

Once these tools have been put in place, it's time to address the root cause of the addiction.
What is it that makes you shop? What do you get out of spending excessively? What triggers you to spend money you don't have?

In a lot of cases, the shopaholic may need to see a doctor or a psychiatrist. They may even need medication, especially if depression or any other mental illnesses are involved.

Once the shopaholic is ready to deal with his or her problem, they can start unravelling any deep-rooted issues that causes them to shop compulsively. This would vary from person to person as people experience trauma differently. Some people could have been neglected as a child and never really worked through it and now shop to feel a part of something.
Others may be shopping to make themselves feel better after a horrible break up. It doesn't matter what the reason is. The important thing is to identify what you're trying to cover up or numb by shopping and address it ASAP.

Conclusion:
Shopping is normal. Shopping compulsively is a problem.
Shopaholics are not seen as bad as those addicted to alcohol or drugs, which fuels the addiction because it's socially acceptable, almost cool.
There are many reasons behind why people shop compulsively, but each person

would have a separate journey as each person would have their own reasons. It is up to us to identify these reasons and start working on them.
The key tool when dealing with a shopping problem is planning.

CHAPTER FIFTEEN
Dealing with a gambling addiction

22:34 Saturday

World famous "pay day" had finally arrived.

Brady and Tash decide to dress up and spoil themselves with a drink or two at an up-market bar in Monte Casino.

"Hey, since we're here, we might as well put a hundred or two on the tables! Come on, we won't even be long!" Brady insists.

Tash doesn't respond, instead she passes on an evil glare that shouts, "NO!"

"Live a little. Jeez!" Brady added, as he walked towards the betting tables.

What is gambling?

Gambling is risking something in hopes that you would get something bigger in return.
Gambling can be very luring, especially with the thought of winning more than you have risked.
You can gamble with pretty much anything: money or material possessions. Hell, you can even gamble away possessions you don't even own as of yet.
For many, gambling is considered to be a fun way to pass time, unfortunately, as with drugs or alcohol, not everyone can gamble successfully.

For those really unlucky ones, they may end up gambling their souls away.

00:35 Sunday

"Dude, you've already made a grand, let's leave!" Tash nags.

Brady ignores her. He's already made a grand and he's on roll.... There's no stopping him now!

He gets up and gets her a double Johnny Walker Blue on the rocks, thinking this should shut her up. She's never had Johnny Walker Blue!

"Oh My God!!" She shouts in excitement. "Okay, we can stay, but just for thirty minutes more."

Gambling Manipulation

Gambling addiction attacks a person's integrity and the gambler can resort to dishonesty, lying, and manipulation.

Compulsive gamblers can be very manipulative, not only to themselves, but to those around them as well.
As with all addictions, the addicts mind convinces them that they need either their substance or addictive behavior for them to function normally, as a result, they do everything in their power to protect their addiction.
Much like how the mind convinces everyone else that they need food and water to survive, the same applies with the mind of a gambler.

I have expanded on the signs of a someone with an addictive personality and why it is that they do what they do in the previous chapter.

Like many other addicts, compulsive gamblers possess the power of persuasion and manipulation.
Unexplainable loans.
One month there's plenty of money with extra to splurge.
The next month, there's barely enough money to pay the rent, let alone debt.
Lying, cheating, stealing, and emotional blackmail becomes the norm.

As most non-gamblers are well aware of how dangerous gambling can be, they often get slack from their closer family and friends. Their actions often covered with long stories that are either sad or completely fictitious.

Something that is also interesting to note is that before the gambler manipulates, lies, or steals from those close to and around him or her, the gambler manipulates themselves first.

'OMG after the hectic month I've had at work, I deserve to spend some money on myself.'

They may try and convince themselves that they don't have a problem or that they just doing it for fun and that they can stop whenever they want. It's their money, it's not like they're hurting anyone, right?
This is the last hundred and I'm going home.
After this, I'm never gambling again.
If I stop now, I have to admit that I am a complete loser.
This highlights that while all of this sounds terrible and it really is, I think it's important to realize that before they lie, cheat, and steal from you, they do it to themselves first. I want to reiterate that. The addict is not doing this to be intentionally malicious, but rather that they are not effectively dealing with a powerful mental disorder that requires for them to lie, cheat and steal to satisfy their craving.

01:12 Sunday

He gets up, not a single chip left, but Tash doesn't have to know that, as far as she knows, he's making a killing, he's just not stopping…" I need the bathroom, I'll be back just now."

"Just hurry the fuck up, I'm becoming annoyed now." Tash moans.

Determined, Brady marches over to the ATM, checking over his back once more to make sure she doesn't see him. There's no way he's leaving this place broke tonight!

With the cash in hand, he still needs the bathroom.

Running to the bathroom, he readies his cards. After having lost a few hundred already, that line of cocaine would do him well.

Signs of a gambler

A gambling addiction is no different to a cocaine addiction. The signs are similar to that of a cocaine addict or an alcoholic.

- The gambler becomes dependent on their harmful behavior and soon starts believing that their body and mind is dependent on the addictive behaviour.

- The gambler experiences great feelings of remorse or guilt after gambling.

- Despite their increased rates of loss, they continue to gamble in hopes that they would recoup all their lost money.

- The gambler experiences signs of depression.

- Loss of sleep

- Loss of control

- When trying to abstain, the gambler becomes restless and irritable.

Compulsive gamblers that have not sought help can worsen already existing addictions.
These addictions may be used to help "escape" the here and now and this can become extremely dangerous. Alcohol, drugs, and other behavioral addictions such as sex is often used when the gambler experiences intense or heightened emotions.

These emotions become a bit much for the gambler and the gambler then resorts, in addition to, their other safety nets. For example, when a gambler has lost a major bet, the intensity can become so overwhelming that they need a drink to calm down.

02:00 Sunday

He made back all his money and an additional 3 grand. Brady couldn't be bothered by entertaining Tash's threats anymore, she has no option but to join in on the excitement now. This doesn't last very long, after a few moments, she insists that they leave again.

He's made so much money, why doesn't he just leave already! This obsessive behavior baffles her.

Denial

The unfortunate truth about compulsive gambler, is that once they have gone too far down and are at the point of protecting their addiction or their security, they can no longer be trusted.

The compulsive gambler is in complete denial about their addiction and refuses to believe that they were outsmarted by their gambling, that they were defeated, and that they can stop anytime they want to.

Very often those that are close to the gambler know that he or she has a problem, but as much as the gambler is in denial, often those close to him are in denial about the gambler's problem as well.

As highlighted previously, gamblers are not necessarily bad people and those close to the gambler often want to trust them because they knew the person before the slots or poker table came into play. They desperately WANT to trust people that can't be trusted. They would know and believe that the gambler has an issue much sooner than the gambler does, they just don't want to believe it. The difficulty with trusting people that can't be trusted is that you may actually be doing the person more harm by enabling them.

02:21 Sunday

"Dude, I've got a long day, I'm out. Will you be able to get home safely?"

"Yeah, don't stress, I'm going to leave soon as well," he responds.

He lost 400 of the 3500 he just made. Still up though.

"Okay, Brady, 20 more minutes and we're cashing up and going home," he thinks to himself.

Winners know when to stop, addicted gamblers don't.

The Compulsive gambler fully believes that he or she can stop whenever they see fit. As mentioned previously, the gambling addict manipulates him or herself before they manipulate others.

Before we go on, let's get one thing straight. While the gambler may not be understood by most non-gamblers, the average gambler is much smarter than the average person and they often have I.Qs well over 120.
Their intelligence acts to their own detriment though. Their first few big wins can actually encourage the thought that they may be smarter than other gamblers or that they may have found a way to make gambling work for them.

Effects of gambling

Compulsive gamblers become so pre-occupied with gambling that they think about gambling even when they're not gambling.

Just have a look at any of the major cell phone app stores, the virtual slot games have amongst the highest downloads. Even though these games aren't necessarily real, they provide that casino gambling feel that so many people are hooked on. Since a lot of gamblers are so pre-occupied with thoughts of gambling, many other areas in their life start falling short. It is common for the addicted gambler to completely neglect themselves and not bathe for days on end.

Financial risks

Gamblers can take out loans to support their habits, borrow money from close friends and family, and often do not have enough money to pay the rent.

The problem is that most gamblers have experienced that "big win" and convince themselves that if they can win again, replacing all that lost money will be easy. Very few are successful though and those that are, end up gambling their winnings away. Their jobs are impacted; often "calling in sick" to gamble. Some gamblers may resort to theft or fraudulent activities to try and support their habit.

Family problems

Friends and family closest to the gambler are often greatly affected by the gambler's actions. Due to constant arguments, marriages fall apart. The gambler starts missing important milestones, important events, and family gatherings. Children in the household become more susceptible to substance abuse or bad grades because their mom or dad is never around, abusive, or provides a negative home environment.

Psychological and physical effects

As mentioned, many gamblers resort to other addictive behaviors or substances to deal with the shame and guilt of their addiction, which can have severe physical consequences. The gambler can suffer from fatigue, high blood pressure, and numerous other physical illnesses.
On top of that, the suicide rates of gamblers are higher than those addicted to drugs.

Compulsive gambling can also lead to cases of severe depression, cross addiction, anxiety, low self-esteem, and many other mental illnesses for as long

as the addiction is not dealt with.
Gambling is incredibly dangerous, but few gamblers are willing to admit they have a problem and only start giving in to the idea once the effects become more obvious and near impossible to hide.

If the gambler is willing to be honest with him or herself from an early stage, then the addiction can be treated, with hopefully as little consequences as possible.

04:06 Sunday

It's gone. It's all gone! Damnit!!
Why didn't he just leave with Tash, he thinks to himself.
Had he left then, he would have walked away with so much extra cash. Annoyed with himself, he walks back to the ATM, withdrawing double the amount he withdrew earlier.
He doesn't have time to play small anymore.
Time is no longer on his side.

Win big or go home, he tells himself.

Gambling to cover the pain

The gambler gets to the point of desperation. This can happen when they are either on a winning or a losing streak.

They start doubling down on bets. They place bets even when he or she have that gut feeling their hand won't win. This is when it becomes increasingly dangerous.

How to treat an active gambling addiction

As with all addictions, the key to recovery is abstinence.
Many can consider going to a rehabilitation centre, provided they receive psychological treatment, well after they left the centre.

The addict can only do this once they have admitted they have a problem and once they have started working on the shame and guilt often built up as a result of the addiction.
Continued denial will only work to the gambler's detriment and all treatment measures will fail.
Not all people have the luxury of affording treatment centres or costly therapy sessions:

Gamblers Anonymous is very effective for those that don't have the financial means to get to a treatment centre.
As they understand the importance of working with like-minded people and working on the underlying issues behind the addiction, such as resentments and fears, as well as making amends to those the gambler has harmed.

For more information check out their site http://www.gamblersanonymous.org for more information on the available help and support groups closest to you.

I would personally recommend that you become actively involved in Gamblers Anonymous and seek professional help as well, in the form of therapy or counselling, even if you have gone to a rehabilitation centre.
The addict in distress can turn to spirituality. Addiction is seen as a spiritual disease and is often linked to spiritual emptiness.
Very often the addict in distress resorts to addiction to fill a spiritual void. Filling this void with healthy spirituality can go a long way in ensuring freedom from addiction.

Many have successfully managed to overcome their gambling addiction through spiritual means and seek to God for help with their addiction. This is incredibly effective, but it is also provided that the person also deals with their underlining psychological issues that contributed to their addiction.

08:30 Sunday

Still in a state of trance, he steps out of Monte casino, the bright light of the sun blinds him.

He started with 200, had he left at 1am, he would have made a profit of 3500 bucks. Right now though, he maxed out his credit cards, with barely enough of his salary remaining to pay this month's rent.

Driving to Cash Converters, he determined. All he needs to do is pawn his TV and surely, he will make most of the money back.

As we have learned in this section of the book, the disease of addiction is universal.
Addiction does not discriminate. What's more scary, is that we are all susceptible to the disease of addiction.

Making Progress

For those that are suffering with the disease of addiction, I hope that you have found this section helpful. For those of you that aren't addicts, I trust that you have found the information helpful and that you have gained a better understanding of addiction, how it affects the addict and why addicts behave the way they do. Use this information to best understand and help those closest to you that suffer with the disease of addiction.

Now we move on to the juicy part of this book. The long awaited, "how-to" section.
In the next section, we will look at practical ways of dealing with some of life's most difficult problems.

PART THREE – LIFE'S LESSONS – A PRACTICAL GUIDE

CHAPTER SIXTEEN
How to deal with life's problems

Here's a shocking little truth:
Life consists of a series of problems.

Yeah, you read right. Life is one big problem, one after the next.

Some problems may seem easy to solve and others are more difficult. More difficult because the solution is not always clear to us and requires a lot of introspection.
Whether we like it or not, we must start working on these problems if we are ever going to hope for a better and happier life.

The types of problems we are faced with.

Shocking little truth number 2:
Odds are that you are not the only one experiencing problems right now.

Yes, everybody is faced with problems. People deal with problems daily, it's really not something that can be escaped.
The only thing that sets some people apart from others is how they deal with these problems.
Some problems may be easier for us to solve and some problems may seem like an impossible nightmare.

Let's take some time to discuss the types of problems we're faced with.

After doing a bit of research and from my personal experience, I found that the below problems seems to be the more common issues and they include:

1. Family problems
2. Feeling that there is not enough time left at the end of the day
3. Problems with finance
4. Their physical and mental health need serious improvements *and*
5. A big one - not being happy where they work.

These are the more obvious, "everyday problems" and are very generalized. As the previous chapters suggest, when it comes to all problems, I insist on digging deeper to truly unravel the problem.

What about those problems that people struggle to talk about? How do we deal with these issues?

For the sake of this part of the chapter, let's say someone was sexually molested. This person blames themselves for the molestation. They feel deep resentment. They have feelings of shame, guilt, anger, and all other negative feelings that you could imagine.
They may feel that by dealing with this issue, it would open them up to more pain and hurt.

It's understandable how this can be very tough to talk about. I think we can both agree that we do not blame this person for not wanting to talk about it either, right?
How then, do they dig deep and explore these issues with a therapist or even a close friend?

Let's briefly explore why we don't like dealing with our problems:

Why we don't like dealing with our problems

The solution seems clear: deal with our problems and they will no longer come back to haunt us, right?
Well, if it's all that clear and simple, then why do we not deal with our problems?

We don't like dealing with our problems for many reasons, which we will go through below.

1. It may be too difficult to deal with, either emotionally or physically.

Consider this: *why do most employers insist on hiring someone with experience?* That's because the more experienced employee will probably be best equipped for the job. Given his prior experience, this employee would most likely have been faced with similar challenges and therefore know how to best deal with

Making Progress

whatever tasks are required.
The more experienced employee is more likely to have been faced with the same challenge over and over again. They are therefore more likely to be able to solve similar problems in shorter periods of time.
The same applies to dealing with problems.
The more experience we have with something, the easier it is to solve.
Fearing something you don't know how to deal with is also completely normal.
The only way we will get better at dealing with our problems is through practice.
It's as simple as that.

2. We may not understand the problem we are faced with.

Ever have that feeling where you know something feels wrong, but can't quite place your finger on it?
You feel like something is bugging you, but you just don't know what it is?
Maybe, just maybe, there aren't any problems. Of course, this is not always the case, but sometimes we look for problems that don't even exist!
Yeah, sometimes we insist on fixing something that is not even broken.

3. We may not be ready to let go and feel that we would be forced to forgive someone that has wronged us.

Often, you would find that you actually **want** to hold onto your problems.
Holding onto your problems can give you a false sense of power. There may even be times when we would need to forgive someone in order for us to deal with our problems. And we may not be ready to "forgive and forget" just yet.

4. By dealing with your problem, it could open up the door to even more problems.

You can easily identify these types of problems by simply identifying what you may have been **suppressing**.
These are the problems we try and bury, in hopes that it goes away.
Well, here's another little shocking truth:
Those problems aren't going anywhere; in fact, it only gets worse with time.

There are a lot of reasons why we avoid dealing with those types of problems.
Usually they link to a lot of emotions, like shame, fear, guilt, remorse, or anger and we feel that by us dealing with these issues, we would open a wounded scar we do not know how to heal.
One of the most troubling thoughts we face with these problems is that once the wound has been revealed, we fear that we would not be able to heal it.

Making Progress

Why we should start facing our problems:

Nadia's story:

With the lights turned off, Nadia sits in her bed, her knees curled up to her forehead, shaking violently. She starts to sob, but knows she has to do it quietly, or else someone may hear her, and ask that horrible question: "WHAT'S WRONG?"
She doesn't know how she will ever forgive herself for what she's done.

It's 23:12 and the house is calm.
Tossing and turning, she tries to fall asleep. Her efforts are in vain, her mind more active than ever.
Quietly, she gets dressed and sneaks out of the house, hoping no one will see her. She can't take this anymore, she has to leave the house.
Driving to the nearest bar, she orders two tequilas and downs them, one after the other...the calm arrives. She feels amazing, has a few more shots, and at 02:32 she leaves the bar, forgetting that she even had any major problems in the first place.

Running late, she eventually arrives at work at 09:37.
She had an important meeting with a client that day. After smelling the alcohol that oozed from her breath, her boss asked her to go home and she does just that.
As if she didn't have enough on her plate, she now has to deal with even more problems at work.

With the lights turned off, Nadia sits in her bed, her knees curled up to her forehead, shaking violently.

Refusing and not being willing to deal with a problem, does not make that problem go away, in fact, it makes the problem bigger and because our behaviors are fear based, we can often add additional problems to our already existing ones.

I bet that one of your goals right now is to live a happy and serene life?
By us not solving or being *willing* to solve these problems, we will never be able to truly reach that state of bliss. Leaving problems unresolved can lead to a lot of physical and mental health issues. It's these very problems that are the cause of our anxiety, stress, and eventually lead too much worse.

We feel shitty about ourselves and this starts having an impact on our relationships, on those closest to us. We start losing sight of what's important to us. Our problems begin to define us. We need to start dealing with our problems to discover what we can learn and use that to grow.

How to deal with problems

So, here's the final shocking truth: There is no magic formula to dealing with problems.

As mentioned, the only way to master the art of dealing with problems is through practice.

Before we go into what can be done to deal with our problems, I need to mention one key ingredient required for us deal with any problem, WILLINGNESS.

Let's begin.
First, we need to be willing to change our mindset.
Once we learn to stop looking at all of our challenges as PROBLEMS, but rather LEARNING CURVES, we become a lot more comfortable when it comes to dealing with our problems. Once we start seeing this as an opportunity for us grow and develop, we lose a lot of the fear we associate with "problem solving."

What I found works best for me is to write everything down before I start working on "fixing" anything.
Here are the below questions you need to ask yourself:

- Is there really a problem? If there is one, what is the problem – Do I truly understand the problem at hand? This must be very specific.
Remember the golden rule, dig deep.

- How does this make me feel? – Yeah, I know it may sound a little cliché, but understanding how a problem makes you feel is incredibly important when trying to solve a problem.
Here you can identify what emotions the problem brings up for you and you can start seeing how it impacts your life. Does it bring anger or sadness in your life? Do you feel overwhelmed by fear because of this problem? Write down any emotions this problem brings up for you.

- Challenges around the problem – write down what makes the problem so difficult. The key here is to be realistic. Understand that there are some things that you can change, some things that may be harder to change, and some things that cannot be changed.
List everything that you can change and everything that cannot be changed.
The next part is to come to accept everything that cannot be changed. Refer to chapter on acceptance if you need a refresher on the power of acceptance and how to accept something.

- What are your goals for solving this problem?
  Why are you trying to solve this problem? What are you hoping to achieve by solving this problem, check these and make sure they are in line with your expectations listed in point 3 in the reasons why people struggle to deal with their problems.

- Think up solutions
  Have a variety of solutions, not just the obvious or most ideal solution. Think of numerous ways to solve this problem.
  Having many solutions to a problem is helpful because when your preferred solution does not work out, you find comfort knowing that there are other solutions.

Having the list above is all good and well, but we want to ensure that you are set for the best chances of success, right?

Focus on the below, and solving your problems becomes so much easier.

It's very important for you to establish what **your** problems are vs what's not your problem.
Sometimes, we take on someone else's problem and this leaves us feeling overwhelmed. It's good to help people, provided we are in a position to help. If, by helping someone, we are taking on more stress than we can handle, then helping this person works to our detriment.

Many of us struggle and feel we are obliged to help other people.
Two things apply in these instances:
1. Try and understand why you have the "need" to help people. Do you long for that feeling of *being* needed, or does it provide you with a sense of power, knowing that someone is dependent on you for help?
2. I have mentioned that problems are learning curves and experiences we can use to grow and learn from.
When you take on someone else's problem, you are depriving that person of growth.
Very often, when we take on other people's issues, we end up doing more harm than good.

Check your own expectations.
I found myself disappointed with who I am and where I am today. The reason for this, is because I had very high expectations for myself.
What's worse is that I did not even know what these expectations were.
I beat myself up for not having met expectations that I wasn't even able to clearly define. Sounds like madness, does it not?

The problem may still be there, because we kept repeating the same mistakes, expecting different results. That is the very definition of insanity, start by changing your thinking. This is also why step 5 in the beginning of this chapter is so important.

Start focusing on yourself.
This could be applied in two ways.
We may think that someone else has a problem, but find that we have been so focused on someone else, that we fail to see our own shortcomings.
Always reassess the situation and determine where **you** have been falling short and if there is anything you need to do from your side to help make the situation better.
Secondly, we cannot compare ourselves to others, much like we cannot compare our traumatic experiences.
Stop comparing your life experiences or your accomplishments to that of others. You are setting yourself up for failure. Unfortunately, there will always be someone better than you, someone stronger and someone that knows how to deal with difficult situations better than you.

Finally, the last thing to focus on is gratitude.
The gift of gratitude has tremendous advantages. Making a conscious decision to be grateful on a daily basis can help improve our mental health.
When we are grateful, we start becoming happier people. It starts developing our personality in a positive manner.
We become more optimistic, it even increases our self-esteem. Try focusing on everything you have to be grateful for and dealing with our problems becomes that much easier.

CHAPTER SEVENTEEN

How to deal with disappointments

"I can't believe I fell for your crap again!" she cries.

"What are you on about! Like seriously, you need to see a therapist or something, you psycho!" He barks.

"You promised that you would be here for me, yet I was alone. I was alone and scared. And once again, you were nowhere to be found!"

Let's face it. We would all love for our lives to be smooth sailing. Nobody likes having their heart broken, their dreams crushed, or left feeling let down. There will always be things that won't go our way or the way we hoped for.

There will come a time where we will be let down by people or failed opportunities. It's inevitable that we will face disappointments.

Being faced with disappointments is not a bad thing, how we deal with these disappointments though determines our ultimate happiness.

What are disappointments

Let's understand what disappointments are and where this feeling stems from.

Disappointment are an immediate emotional response after a <u>perceived failure</u>.

This primary emotion, disappointment, can manifest itself in many ways. We get angry, hurt, upset, indifferent, despondent, or we feel a combination of these emotions.

At this point, it's somewhat obvious that disappointments can lead to crappy emotions, so let's dig deeper to understand why we really get disappointed.

Disappointments occur when an expectation has not been met. Expectations stem from our beliefs.
Our beliefs stem from our needs.
Okay, I know this may seem a little confusing now, so let's use an example to simplify this:

Wesley longs to feel loved, to feel wanted.

He finally meets the girl of his dreams and after two weeks, they chat like they've known each other for ages. He experiences sensations he forgot existed – after all, he has been single for two years now.
This girl fulfills his need to feel loved, to feel wanted.

Two days later, she phones him and breaks it off. She tells him that she is still madly in love with her ex and that she's not ready for another relationship.

A wave of disappointment rushes over him because she could not fulfil his need to feel loved.
She could not fix his problem of loneliness.

In the above example, we saw poor Wesley falling madly in love with a girl, a girl that he hoped would fix his problem; his need. When she could not fix it, it led to disappointment and all the other negative emotions that followed.

On a deeper level, disappointment reflects our passion towards something. Quickly take some time to think about it. If you didn't care about something then there would be no disappointments. The greater your disappointment, the more passionate you are.
So already, we're seeing the good in disappointments. Our disappointments can help show us what we're really passionate about.

Now that we have a decent understanding of what disappointments are and where they stem from, let's see how our disappointments affect us and how many of us deal with our disappointments.

What happens when we are disappointed?

When faced with disappointments, our perception of the world can become skewed. We feel negative, down, or outright despondent. We fail to see all good around us and solely focus on the bad life has to offer.

If we let it, disappointment can lead us down a horrible path of depression.

Wesley is a recovering alcoholic. He's managed to stay clean of all substances for over a year now.
This relationship, something he has been longing for over a year, would have been one of his gifts of recovery from the universe. This is what he believed when he first entered recovery – Do good and the universe will bless you.

After she left him for her undeserving ex, he decided to numb himself and picked up that first drink.

Had Wesley gone into this new relationship understanding that even though he had a need, people make their own choices and that he will have to be okay with whatever choice she makes, both seen and unforeseen, his disappointment would be much less harsh. His disappointment arose from his expectation of her.

We will go into expectations soon enough. First, let's go through some of the things people do when faced with disappointment.

- **Avoidance**
  Many people will resort to avoidance by numbing themselves with different activities. This would vary from person to person. Some may start gaming excessively. Others may resort to alcohol, drugs, or other addictive behaviors to try numbing themselves. Other people may just shut off from the rest of the world.
  It doesn't matter what avoidance/numbing method is used, none of these activities will resolve the issue. These methods will provide a temporary, false sense of upliftment, but the undealt with problem remains. As we have now established, undealt with problems become harder to manage over time.

- **Pretend their needs don't exist**
  Some people block out their needs and pretend as though they don't exist.
  As time goes on, Wesley believes that his inner need for affection doesn't exist, that he is content being alone. He develops barriers around love, making it hard for anyone else to stand a chance. Deep down, he holds onto a resentment that denies him of any happiness in the future.

- **People give up on their dreams and goals**
  You may have found something that you're passionate about, only to have to it blow up in your face. You weren't able to achieve the results you desperately hoped for. What happens then? You give up on your

dreams. You convince yourself that it was pointless and stupid to even think about it.

While you might have made a conscious decision to give up on your dreams, your subconscious cannot be fooled so easily. It knows your inner desires, your inner passion. It knows that you want nothing more than to be a great writer, that world famous soccer player, or an owner of your own successful business.

Quick reality check – when you deny your dreams, your goals, your deepest needs and desires, you live an empty life – a life with no meaning or purpose.

Avoiding disappointment is bad because they give us the experience we need to learn how to solve little setbacks.
When learning to overcome these setbacks, they become valuable tools when we are faced with more difficult, complex problems.

Optimist vs Pessimist vs Perfectionist

Optimism is very rewarding, it allows you to feel wonderful even though the end result isn't clear. The optimist maintains a positive attitude and strives to remain positive through all times. They are the dreamers, the people that are hopeful.

Optimists have their reasons for choosing to see the world in a positive light, but the danger is that they face even more disappointment than the pessimist. Because they dare to dream, opportunities for disappointment are more prevalent. There are only so many crushing blows this person can handle before they feel defeated.

The pessimist faces disappointment a lot less than the optimist.
If you expect the worst from someone, it's hard to get disappointed.

That does not mean that it's better to be pessimistic, rather than optimistic, to prevent disappointments. Even though the pessimist may seemingly be less disappointed, they are more likely to have a skewed perception of reality. Pessimists see negative events as *permanent* and ultimately, this eats away at their happiness.

Contrary to what many people think, perfectionism is not a good thing.
The Perfectionist lives in a constant state of anxiety. They always focus on what is wrong and as a result they obsess and never feel good enough. When it comes to disappointments, they are their own worst enemy.

We will go into more detail about the importance of understanding your character type at the end of this chapter.

Why Disappointments are good for you

While there's a lot of negatives, let's focus on the positives of dealing with expectations. Once we understand and see the positives that disappointments provide us with, managing our disappointments becomes a lot easier.

1. Disappointments teach us to manage our expectations.
   Often we have expectations of others or of ourselves. When these expectations fall short, we feel disappointed. Disappointments allows us to redefine our expectations and to make them more reasonable and realistic.

2. It teaches us a lot about ourselves.
   It can teach you what pushes your buttons.
   It teaches us what makes us tick, what makes us sad, what hurts us, and what makes us angry.
   They also show us how we handle hurt, rejection, frustration, and anger. Understanding these underlying issues is key to dealing with our problems.

3. It shows you what really matters to you.
   Remember, the greater the disappointment, the more passionate you are about something.

4. It can motivate us to try harder.
   The difference between an average salesman and a great salesman, is that the great salesman does not give up, even after being faced with endless rejection and disappointment. They persevere and find new ways of making sales until they succeed. A great salesman is faced with a lot more disappointment than the average guy.

5. It teaches us to know when to stop pursuing something.
   Pursuing something does not necessarily mean that you will get it. Unfortunately, some things are not meant to be. Disappointments can help us identify which of these things we should stop pursuing. When we stop pursuing these things, it leaves us with more energy for new possibilities that can open new doors.

Disappointment is a trouble shooting tool which allows us to assess our perception of reality. While the feeling of disappointment is negative, it is always a better emotional state than apathy or indifference. The ability to feel makes us

human.
Treasure that feeling.

How to deal with Disappointments

While being disappointed is completely normal and healthy, that is not to say that we should now go out and look for opportunities to get disappointed. Too much disappointment is bad.

The more we face disappointment, the more unhappy, unmotivated, and stressed we become.
Being faced with constant disappointment in our selves will affect our self-esteem.
Being constantly disappointed with certain aspects of our relationships will affect the relationship. In fact, this is one of the biggest reasons people get divorced.
It is therefore crucial that we learn to deal with our disappointments in a positive manner and implement strategies to reduce our disappointments in the future.

Before we move on to dealing with expectations, let's quickly revisit the importance of understanding our personality type.

Understanding our personality type helps us find which areas concern us and what we need to remain cognisant of when working through our disappointments.

The optimist sees disappointments as temporary, but because they are big dreamers and live on hope, it is crucial for them to adjust their expectations. Their expectations need to be more realistic to help prevent disappointment in the future.

The pessimist sees disappointments as permanent. They need to continually remind themselves that disappointments and setbacks are only temporary. They also need to look at each problem as an isolated and specific event, rather than adding to their already existing problems, which creates the belief that the world is a bad place.

The perfectionist believes that life is perfect and in turn, *they* should be perfect. They create unrealistic expectations that are deemed to fail, leading to disappointment. The Perfectionist would have to dig deeper to understand their need to always have things "perfect." Perfectionism doesn't just happen. It's often a result of a false belief that nothing they do is good enough.

Once you've identified the personality type that is most applicable to you, you know what areas to focus on most.
Now we can begin to address our disappointment.

Whenever we face disappointments, we are in a state of sadness, fear, grief, or apathy. When we are in this state, our thinking is flawed. We don't think clearly and logically.

Step 1

The first step is to clear this negative state of being and aim for a more neutral and positive state. Try finding positive activities that can help you recharge. Do something that makes you feel better.

This may even be spending alone time or finding positive activities that will help you feel better, such as painting, or whatever you enjoy.

It's crucial to manage your emotions. Try your hardest not to make any big decisions while being in this emotional state. What I found helps me, is reminding myself that I am in a temporary emotional state and therefore need to tread carefully, watch what I say, and how I act. The last thing you want is to create more problems for yourself by acting out while you're in this emotional state.

Step 2

The second step is to self-reflect. Once we're in a more positive state, we need to self-reflect. This will help us understand where we went wrong, what really hurt or upset us, and what we can do to manage our expectations better in the future.

The ability to self-reflect is the essence of good mental health.

<u>1) Become of aware of your expectations.</u>

What are the expectations you are creating?

Disappointments results from our expectations not being met. Sometimes these expectations are clear and obvious. Often, we are disappointed because of unspoken expectations. These are expectations we expect people to fulfil, without voicing that these are what we're expecting or hoping for.

<u>2) Understand your beliefs behind the expectation.</u>

What needs drive these expectations and why it is important to you to have these expectations met?

Do your expectations need to be voiced?
Do your expectations need to be adjusted?
Are these expectations unrealistic or unreasonable?
Are there other ways that your needs could be met?

Step 3

Action plan

After self-reflecting, it's time to take all that information and turn it into something positive. Use this time to come up with a plan to move forward. This step is really important, because if left un-dealt with, the disappointment could turn into resentment. Take all the answers from Step 2, and use this information to draft a plan going forward. This plan will help reduce your disappointments and manage your expectations better.

We all make mistakes, what really counts is that we learn from these mistakes. We must allow ourselves time to heal, this is not an overnight process.

Once we have practiced the art of acceptance and sought help when needed, we make new plans and open ourselves up to new opportunities.
This is how we learn and grow from our disappointments.

Finally, as hard as it may be, don't tell people about what "might happen." Share your joy and success after it happens. You read about this in many business and self-development books. When we tell people about our *potential successes,* we put a lot of unnecessary pressure on ourselves. When we do not live up to these expectations, we are left feeling like failures.

In conclusion, disappointments are normal. They can be very hurtful, numbing, and painful, but when channelled correctly, they can be incredible tools for growth.

CHAPTER EIGHTEEN
How to forgive and forget

"I'm such a fool! I can't believe I fell for your lies again!" Mandy screams.

"Please just hear me out. I am so sorry." John sobs.

"Take your stuff and get out! Get out! I don't ever want to see you or that useful mother of yours in my house ever again. LEAVE!"

Anger. Pain. Hurt. Despair. Holding onto grudges. Deep and dark resentments.

Quickly, look back up and read the conversation between Mandy and John again. Do you see how harmful this is, not only for the person that hurt her, but for herself as well?
What emotions does this bring up for you?
Does it bring up fear?
Perhaps you sense a feeling of anger?
Perhaps you can even relate to it right now and it brings up something personal for you?

You may have been in search of inner peace and happiness, but cannot remember the last time you were actually happy.

If any of this resonates with you, then chances are, you may need to learn the art of forgiveness.

Why people don't forgive?

FACT: Unless you were born as a robot, forgiveness is tough and resentment is natural.

Before we start discussing how one can forgive, let's spend some time going over why people DON'T forgive…

Very simply, people hold onto anger, because they get something out of it. Whether it's on a conscious or subconscious level, there is always an advantage for holding onto anger and resentment.

I personally fear forgiveness for many reasons.
Holding onto grudges and resentments, has, for a very long time, been a defense mechanism. Often, I would feel that I have been hurt too much and that by forgiving, I would be letting the person off the hook.
This seems somewhat obvious, so let's dig a bit deeper:

"Oh, shame. He really has been through so much. I honestly don't blame him for behaving the way he does."

Holding on to grudges for me, came with a certain feeling of "being right." Letting go of that anger would mean I lost that power. Also, being the one that has been *wronged*, I get to play the victim.
Long story short, by playing the victim, I get to look for compassion and attention from others.
I can complain about my difficulties and others will listen.
Why? Well, because I deserve special attention. More importantly, because I was wronged, my own wrongful behaviors are automatically excused.

I think it is clear that by holding onto our anger, although it's natural, we definitely get something out of it. As mentioned in the beginning of the chapter, by holding onto hurt and anger, it hurts not only the person that should be forgiven, but it hurts you as well.

Quickly take a few moments to think of any areas where you're struggling to forgive someone. Think about what you stand to gain by holding onto that resentment?

Why should we forgive?

Resentments do not serve their purpose.
Apart from the above-mentioned reasons, we hold onto them, because subconsciously this is our way of defending ourselves. We hold onto grudges because we hope that it would help us feel better and hopefully heal, by keeping the other person at bay.

Why should we forgive others that have hurt us though?
There are a few important points that we will now go through to understand why forgiveness is important:

- Holding onto anger hurts you more than the other person.

- Forgiveness is not for the other person. Forgiveness is for you.

- Forgiving someone does not make that person's actions or even their behavior okay.

- By holding onto grudges, you start losing sight of everything else that is good around you.

- Forgiveness can lead to understanding.

Holding onto anger hurts you more than the other person. Chances are the other person has continued living life. They may or may not have felt any remorse for their actions, probably have found a way to move on. They have moved on and you're still stuck in a vicious cycle of hate.

Are the advantages of holding onto grudges really that great?
Do you not long for the benefits of forgiveness like less stress, less mental problems, or feeling like a heavy weight has been lifted off your shoulders? Wouldn't it be great if you could claim that you are happy and really mean it? Think about it.
It's important that you do, because only once you start realizing all the benefits that come with forgiveness, do you start realizing that you are actually not forgiving the other person for their sake. You are forgiving them for yourself. You are forgiving the person that has wronged you, because you deserve a happy, healthier, stress free life.

A major misconception with forgiveness, is that by forgiving someone, this means that you need to tolerate his or her behavior again.
Again. Forgiveness is not for the other person, it is for yourself.
It is perfectly normal to forgive someone, but keep your distance from them.
Forgiveness is the act of letting go, not going back for more hurt and pain.

Sometimes, it may be much harder to forgive.
Perhaps irreversible damage was made.
Perhaps you lost a loved one because of someone else's mistake. Perhaps someone stole a valuable or sentimental jewel you will never be able to regain.

Here's the harsh reality:

What's done is done. What's gone is gone.
As much as it hurts, it simply cannot be reversed. You have two options though:

1. You live without what you have been deprived of and live a life with anger, resentment, and pain for the remainder of your life.

2. You live without what you have been deprived of and start living a life, filled with fulfilling spiritual values, free of anger, and of inner peace.

Forgiveness can lead to understanding. Often, we are so clouded by our anger that we don't take the time to try and understand the situation.
We may be unwilling to speak to the other person, to hear their point of view. Think about how many times you realized that you were angry at someone without actually understanding the whole situation? We might just find that the other person has a valid reason for doing what they did. They may even have so much remorse that forgiving them becomes easier for us to do.

How to forgive?

So, I've pointed out all the benefits of forgiveness, but that leaves us with the question,

With all that betrayal and hurt I went through, how do I forgive?

I tried searching for answers, I have asked people, I have checked on the web and felt that all my search attempts were in vain. After all my search attempts, I could not find a blue print to guarantee success at forgiving.
Guess what?...It doesn't exist.

As mentioned, forgiveness is not easy, but there are certain steps that can be taken, starting NOW.

Firstly, we must make the decision to let go.
By us weighing the pros and cons of holding onto our anger, we come to realize that this anger does us more harm than good. When we decide to make the decision to try and let go, to the best of our ability, that important, problem solving, key comes into play - WILLINGNESS.
We understand that it may not be easy, but we are willing to do whatever it takes for us to achieve that inner peace we know we deserve.

Once we are willing to try and forgive, we can then attempt the below two steps (note that it has to be in this order in order for it be effective):

1. Forgive YOURSELF.
2. After forgiving yourself, you can then start forgiving the other person

We may or may not realize it, but a lot of the anger we hold onto is not entirely aimed at the person who hurt us. It is often aimed at ourselves.

By us holding onto that anger and resentment, it serves as a method for us to punish ourselves.

We may think that we were incredibly stupid or silly for having let that person hurt us. This may not have been the first time we have been hurt. We may think that we were naïve in placing our trust in someone so obviously untrustworthy.

Rather than focusing on all the negatives we're faced with, try changing your perspective.
Focus on positives, even though it may seem limited.
Focus on what lessons can be learned.
Focus on the growth you have displayed over the years.
Think back to when you had a difficult situation and how you were able to overcome it.
Focus on why you deserve inner peace and happiness.

Forgiveness is an act of strength and improves your self-esteem tremendously when done right.

I cannot emphasize this enough. We forgive people, not for them, but because we are deserving of that forgiveness.
Forgive yourself and forgiveness for others will follow.

CHAPTER NINETEEN

Understanding and dealing with resentments

Resentments are like drinking poison and waiting for the other person to die.
– AA Fellowship.

What are resentments?

A resentment is a grudge you hold onto after being hurt by someone.

It occurs when a person has ongoing anger or hatred towards another person because of an injustice, regardless of whether it's real or imagined.

The person holding onto the resentment may feel victimized, but their anger, fear, or shame doesn't allow them to discuss the resulting emotions. They allow the grudge to fester and be expressed in a form of anger or hatred.
These people build an alarming desire for revenge.

Before we go on, it's important to understand that anger is a healthy emotion. Contrary to what a lot of people may think, anger is completely normal and should never be suppressed. How we express that anger though, determines whether it's healthy or not.

Anger is an emotional response to an injustice. Holding onto that anger is unhealthy and that is when a resentment starts to form.

In a nutshell, resentments result from an inadequate expression of emotions after a painful experience.

Resentment is a fear-based emotion that eats away at our happiness. Resentments waste away time that could have been spent with love and joy.

Resentment, anger, and fear are all connected.

I think it's clear that holding onto resentments only seem to have a negative impact.
The question we need to ask ourselves is, *Why do we insist on holding onto resentments?*

Holding onto a resentment serves as a way of punishing yourself or another person. We punish the other person for hurting us and we punish ourselves for allowing the hurt.

The effects of resentments

The effects of holding onto resentments can be crippling. Holding onto a resentment can significantly damage your ability to interact with the world.

By holding onto a resentment, you are only hurting yourself.
We may think that we are harming the other person, but the real person we hurt is ourselves.

Ultimately, by holding onto resentments, it adds more stress and anxiety in our life. Stress and anxiety that is not necessary.

The key to dealing with resentments is forgiveness.
This has been discussed in detail in the previous chapter, but we will quickly go through the importance of forgiveness when we assess how to deal with resentments shortly.
When someone is unable to forgive, mental problems begin to arise.

If you are holding onto resentments, you also stand a risk of developing a skewed perception of life.
Unresolved resentments can cause someone to feel like a victim in every situation.
Once you've reached the point of always playing the victim, finding any positive outcomes in life becomes increasingly difficult.

Finally, feelings of anger and rage can lend a false sense of power.
If you are enraged or clinging onto a resentment, this could cause you to falsely believe that you hold power over the other person. This is especially true if the other person keeps pushing for your forgiveness.

Remember, when holding onto resentments, the only person you hurt is yourself.

How to deal with resentments

Resentment wastes time and happiness. Time that could have been spent with love and joy.

When you realize that happiness is an inside job, you are less likely to look for happiness elsewhere. Keep this thought in mind when learning to deal with your resentments.

Dealing with a resentment is not easy. It becomes even harder to deal with if you hold onto many, because at this stage, you may have developed that skewed perception of reality and feel you cannot trust anyone.

Apart from all the false benefits, there's a reason why you have developed your resentments, and that is because you felt that you were truly hurt or harmed.

While resolving resentment is not easy, there are a few things that can be done to assist in dealing with your resentments.

Below are a few things to consider before attempting to deal with your resentments.

Understand that by choosing to deal with your resentments, you're embarking on a long and painful journey.
Remember that these resentments did not build up overnight. It does not make any sense for you to think that you can rid yourself of these resentments in a short period of time.

This could be a painful journey, but the destination is completely worth it.

That being said, it's important to note that unveiling the hurt of your past will leave you feeling worse before you feel any better.

Forgiveness

One of the most important tools you need to develop is the art of forgiveness. Developing an ability to forgive is important as well as acknowledging the feelings underneath the resentment.

When you let go of resentment, you are not condoning their actions, instead you are doing it to allow yourself to be free from the heaviness of carrying it around.

Forgiveness is hard, but it becomes easier when you have developed high self-confidence.
This brings us to the next point.

Self-esteem

In life, we will always face judgment and criticism. Even if we are complete hermits, somebody will have something negative to say about us.

We decide how we are going to handle the criticism.
If someone tells me that I am the size of a Hippo and I allow it to affect me personally, this could serve as a sign that I am not comfortable with my weight.

By dealing with resentments, it allows us to assess areas in our life; where we fall short and are what we're not comfortable with.

It also gives us an opportunity to focus on ourselves, rather than the mistakes of others.

Give without expectations

We often do things for people, but don't actually realize that we are doing it with unspoken expectations. When people do not live up to our expectations, we then develop resentments towards them. In every situation, check your motives and expectations.

Ask yourself:
What's in it for me?
Is there anything in it for me?
Am I doing something in hopes that the favor will be returned?"

Gratitude

Harness the power of gratitude.
With gratitude, we realize that in life, we cannot always have things our way and that's okay.
We focus on what we have, rather than what we don't.

Gratitude is crucial for reaching a state of inner peace.

Stay open to different outcomes

Know that just by choosing to work through your resentments, this does not mean that you will always have a positive outcome or that things will work out as you have expected.

When dealing with your resentments, you would often find favorable outcomes, but there will be times when the results are not what you have hoped for. Remain cognisant of this before dealing with any resentment.

What NOT to do.

Before we learn how to deal with our resentments, let's briefly cover a few **NOT TO DO** points:

1. Do NOT ignore your resentments
2. Do NOT pretend they don't exist – The "fake it until you make it" approach, is not effective when it comes to dealing with resentments
3. Do NOT fight through them – trying to believe that resentments do not have a negative impact on your life can do more harm than good. Undealt with resentments will eventually suffice, whether returning with a wave of sadness or physically lashing out because of your frustrations.
4. Do NOT try and forget them.

Guide to dealing with resentments

Steps to follow to effectively deal with resentments:

1) Identify all people you have resentments towards.

Remember that nothing is too *small*. It's important to list each and every person, concept, or institution that you feel has harmed you in any way and caused you to hold onto anger as a result thereof.

What many people do is only focus on the bigger, more obvious resentments they hold onto. Avoid only focusing on the *bigger* resentments.
It's essential that you deal with all resentments to truly free yourself.

2) Establish what they did to hurt you

The next step is to write down why you resent this person.
This is the part where things may get worse before they get better. This part of

the exercise requires you to dig deep and as a result, you may feel exposed. Your emotions will be raw. This is generally the case if you do not know how to deal with these emotions. During this phase, you will prove to yourself that you can *sit through* difficult emotions and come out okay.

3) Write down each aspect of your life that this resentment affects.

Self-confidence, trust issues, etc. The point of this step is to become aware of how these resentments affect your ability to trust, to feel safe, to feel secure, and feel loved.

4) Write down how you contributed towards this resentment.

This step is crucial. We don't often realize how we contributed towards our own resentments. We often just assume that we had no role in whatever happened.
Did we have unrealistic expectations?
Does this person know that we are holding resentments towards them?
Did we contribute in any way to what actually happened?
Do we know the full story before declaring our hatred towards this person?

When you're done with this list, speak to someone you hold in high regard about your resentments.
Very often, an outside perspective can help you see things that may cloud your anger.

This method is commonly used in the various "anonymous" meetings and has proven very successful for a lot of people.
While this does not guarantee you will rid yourself of resentments, it can certainly go a long way towards giving yourself freedom from all the anger and hurt you've been holding onto.

CHAPTER TWENTY

Jealousy - a sign of insecurity

You scoop around, checking messages on their phone when they are not watching.
Your compliments are insincere and you only pretend to be happy for them.
You criticize them and try humiliating them whenever you find the opportunity.
Perhaps there is that one person that reminds you of how you messed up in the past, or you just hate.

If any of the above resonates with you, then you may be **jealous**.

What is jealousy?

Jealousy is a complex emotion that usually presents itself in two main forms:

- When you are about to lose something that is very important to you.

- When someone else has done something and this brings up feelings of anger, hurt, or even hatred.

The first type of jealousy is easy to identify in relationships. You may suspect that your partner is cheating on you and the fear of losing your partner (someone that is very dear to you), causes you jealousy.

The second type is closely linked to envy. It's important to note that there's a clear difference between envy and jealousy.

<u>Jealousy</u>

When somebody has something that you don't have or they have done something that you couldn't, resulting in a negative state of mind.
When it brings up emotions like resentment, hurt, anger, or hatred, you could be faced with jealousy.

Envy

When somebody has something, or has something you don't have, but want, or want to do.
Envy can actually be healthy. You may admire a close friend's ripped muscles and be envious of their beach body. And then, you ask him what his secret is – that is an example of envy.

> *Jealousy is no more than feeling alone against smiling enemies. –Elizabeth Bowen.*

Jealousy does not pose a major block on our personal and emotional wellbeing. Jealousy isn't the problem. The problem is all the other emotions that follow. This includes feelings of: loss, insecurity, fear, abandonment, hurt, anger, and hatred.
Jealousy brings about very destructive emotions.

WHAT CAUSES JEALOUSY

Like all other problems, jealousy, in itself, is not the problem. The problem is the driving factors behind jealousy.
What are the underlying problems behind our feelings of jealousy?

I have broken it down into 6 main sub-categories, as per below:

Possessiveness

Possessive people are those that don't like sharing what is dear to them with others. When the possessive person feels like something that belongs to them is being taken away or even being shared, feelings of hurt and jealousy develop.

Co-dependence

Co-dependent people find happiness in others.
This happens a lot when someone has a very low self-esteem and feel that they cannot find happiness within themselves. They find happiness from other people. When it feels like their primary source of happiness is being taken away from them, feelings of jealousy arise.

Low self-esteem

Those that believe there is something wrong with them typically suffer from a low self-esteem.
They struggle to find the good in their actions. They experience constant feelings of inadequacy.
Due to all these insecurities, they also constantly compare themselves to others and by doing so, develop resentments towards other people.
The jealousy is formed because, try as they might, they feel that they can never compare with these people.

Emotional instability

Rapid changes in mood can affect how we perceive things. Feelings of anxiety, fear, and depression have a great impact on how we view the world.
These can all be very big driving factors towards fear-based actions such as insecurity, fear of abandonment, and fear of loss. This ultimately results or contributes to feelings of jealousy.

Resentments

Our past hurt can trigger feelings of jealousy and insecurity, especially if we have not dealt with it effectively.
Those that do not effectively deal with their resentments start believing that history will always repeat itself.
Because we were previously cheated on and have not dealt with it, we may be in a new relationship and find ourselves checking up on our partner's phone to see if they are being honest and faithful.
Unresolved resentment is very dangerous, because if we find that history has in fact repeated itself and that our jealous suspicions came true, we then start blaming ourselves for having fallen for the same lies again or we may start believing that we are the problem.

Shame

The reason why shame is such a big driving factor in addiction is because we may have done something that we have not forgiven ourselves for. The shame becomes so overwhelming that we are constantly "on the run" or trying to escape.
This comes with anxiety and this anxiety follows us in relationships and our dealings with other people. Un-dealt with shame and guilt of our past strongly influences how we act today.
We may have acted in a shameful manner, and as a result, we start feeling that others may behave in a similar manner.

These are the main driving factors behind our jealousy.

When dealing with jealousy, we have to deal with the underlying issues.
We must understand the root cause of this jealousy.

HOW TO OVERCOME JEALOUSY

Imagine living a life filled with feelings of constant suspicion and uncertainties? You start blaming others for your feelings of insecurity. You struggle to believe anyone and are constantly faced with doubts about everything…
Unless jealousy is dealt with, you will either remain or could eventually become this person.

Like all problems, the first step is awareness. Recognizing there is a problem goes a long way in solving it.

Again, remember that when trying to resolve or work on your jealousy, you aren't actually working on jealousy itself. You are working on the underlying psychological issues driving this behavior. The jealousy that will be lifted is a reward of dealing with your buried issues.

First, you need to identify what the driving factors are that are causing you to act jealous.
Are you possessive, co-dependent, or emotionally unstable?
Do you have a low self-esteem, and this causes you unnecessary jealousy?
Are you holding onto shame and resentment that could lead to jealousy?
By dealing with the underlying issue, you then automatically deal with your issues of jealousy.

Working on jealousy can be tough because it requires deep and honest introspection.

It's important to mention that jealousy does not just affect us.
We can either be jealous and need to look within ourselves to start working on it or we could be experiencing the wrath of someone jealous around us.
If you are jealous, chances are that those close to you suffer as a result of your insecurities.

How to deal with jealous people:

> 1) Often, the person may not realize that they are behaving in a destructive or jealous manner and it could all be due to miscommunication. Try speaking to the person and tell them how their actions make you feel.

2) Try not to take it personally. Remember, someone else's jealousy is not about you. It is about them and is something that they need to address.

3) Try reducing the negative interactions you may have with this person. Even though their jealousy is about them, if they are not willing to seek help or start working on their jealousy, it may be difficult to keep them in your life, especially if you are in the process of working on a healthier, more emotionally secure you.
Constant negativity impacts you. Jealousy and all the other negative emotions that stem from it, is contagious.

4) Assess if the person adds value in your life. If the person only brings negativity and only seems to have bad things to say, then it might be necessary to cut that person out of your life.

Final word:

Myth buster: Jealousy is not a sign of love, it is not a sign of care and affection. It's a sign of insecurity.

CHAPTER TWENTY-ONE

Understanding Loneliness and how to fix it

People are interconnected, regardless of race, sex, or nationality. Nobody came into this world alone and for that reason, people long for closeness with others.

Very simply, loneliness can be defined as an unwelcomed isolation. Being alone, not because of our own choosing, but because of circumstances often beyond our control.

Many studies have proven and shown that when answering the question, "What makes people happy?" the answers received, varied. Some people may say that ice cream or pizza makes them happy, others may say that financial and material possessions is the root to their happiness.
What these studies have found is that the most common answer would be the longing of close, happy and healthy relationships.

Social media does not always do what it was intended to do:
bring people together.

How many times have you taken 20 pics of ultimately the same pic, to find that perfect snap?
If I'm going to upload this on Facebook, people must see how awesome I look today!

In today's age of technology, cliques, and social expectations, that "feeling of belonging," proves to be very difficult for a lot of people.
Millions of people, right now, feel like social outcasts.
Social media can actually be intimidating for many. People see pictures of others on Twitter or Facebook and wish they had that person's looks, their friends, or even the car they drive. This constant comparison leaves them feeling inadequate. Many of us want to engage socially, but more of us are struggling because we feel that we will never be as good, as beautiful, or as popular as those we see on Instagram every day.

The truth about loneliness is that, Loneliness has nothing to do with how many friends you have; it's the way you feel inside.

The link with mental health

Anxiety, depression, addiction, and eating disorders: all these mental illnesses have a direct impact on how someone perceives the world, as well as their ability to build healthy and sustainable relationships. The bigger the mental issues are, the bigger the likelihood of isolation, self-shame, lowered self-esteem, and social anxiety.

Nobody understands me or knows how I feel.

The link with physical health

Physical health is a gift that you can only give yourself; a gift that money can't buy. It's common for someone that does not look after his or her physical health to have a lowered self-esteem. Their confidence levels are much lower than the average person. This makes socializing with others, that much harder.

The quality of someone's physical health is very closely linked with loneliness. Someone with poor physical health is more likely to suffer from other mental illnesses, ultimately resulting in the increased likelihood of loneliness.
On the flip side, someone that is currently lonely may start neglecting his or her physical health. They may feel that there is no point in taking care of themselves anymore - nobody really *wants to be around them,* anyway.
They have very little or no healthy sustainable relationships. At least, not the relationships they want.

When someone's mental and physical health deteriorates, that person may not want to be around other people and they'll choose to abstain from all people.

<u>Constantly wanting to be alone can create a self-fulfilling prophecy.</u>

When we constantly want to be by ourselves, we may start believing that people do not want to be around us or that nobody enjoys our company.
A lot of the time, people want to be around us, **we** are the ones that don't want to be around them, yet we blame them for *not being there for us* in our time of need?

Finally, loneliness is contagious. People that are lonely transmit loneliness. Those that spend excessive amounts of time around others that are lonely, become lonely themselves. Remember, loneliness is not about how many people you have around you, it's the way you feel inside.

Let's spend a bit of time digging deeper into the issues around loneliness, starting with the stigma attached to loneliness.

The stigma behind Loneliness

What makes loneliness harder to treat, is the stigma attached to it. Because of this stigma, people are unable to admit their loneliness.

Recent studies have shown that millions of people experience loneliness on a daily basis, yet, few of these people are willing to openly admit their loneliness.

Social media, television, magazines, even those around us can sometimes paint this picture of what an ideal world or what an ideal life would look like. We then either consciously or subconsciously start comparing our own lives to these ideals and more often than not, we find that we fall short of these standards. There are thousands of people suffering without people even knowing, because of the stigma attached to loneliness. This stigma makes admitting our loneliness hard and uncomfortable to admit to ourselves.

Many people would rather openly talk about depression and their other fears before talking about their loneliness. This is because loneliness is seen, by many, as a sign of weakness and people fear that they will be negatively judged by others.

Loneliness is often associated with old age.
Statistically, elderly people can often be lonelier than younger people, because they may not have as much exposure or interaction with others.
This is another stigma that is not always true because loneliness affects all people.
In fact, more and more young people are being affected by loneliness today.
If you're reading this and feeling reminded of your loneliness, just know that you're not alone.

Introvert VS Extrovert

There is a very big misconception that introversion and loneliness are closely linked.
First, let's start by establishing what the primary difference between an introvert and an extrovert is.

> *An Extrovert is someone that appears to be socially confident, friendly, and outgoing?*

> *An Introvert is someone that is shy and prefers to refrain from as much social events as possible?*

On the surface, the above definitions may seem correct and this is how the many people view extroverts and introverts. If this is your current view…then this is not completely accurate.

An introvert can simply be defined as someone that reenergizes by spending quality alone time.

An extrovert can simply be defined as someone that reenergizes by being around people, by connecting with others, and making social contact.

Introverts enjoy spending quality time alone and that is great. In fact, it can even be healthy. That's how the introvert recharges and re-energizes.

The key difference is that the introvert is alone by choice and someone that suffers from loneliness is not alone by choice, but rather by forces, often outside of their control.

Effects of loneliness

When people feel socially accepted and *apart of*, they often function best. That feeling of belonging can greatly contribute to people remaining motivated and having that drive that pushes them to complete their required daily functions.

When these basic social requirements are not met, the consequences can be severe.

Effects of loneliness on children

The effects of loneliness on children can be quite severe. These effects also carry with the child, well into their adulthood.

Unable to connect socially from a young age, can cause a lot of children to develop negative coping mechanisms, such as lying, stealing, or even being manipulative in an attempt to try fit in and be *accepted*.

These kids believe that the world is an evil and cruel place and often believe that they have to fend for themselves at a young age. These kids grow up way too fast and often skip the important early developmental stages of childhood.

A lot of kids turn to drugs, alcohol, sex or even join street gangs in an attempt to escape that overwhelming feeling of loneliness.

Effects of loneliness in adults

With adults, the effects of loneliness can be very bad as well. Loneliness is a major contributing factor for depression. Lonely adults are more likely to turn to alcohol, drugs, and sex to fill that void; that feeling of *emptiness*.

Lonely adults are known to be under a lot more stress than those with healthy relationships.
They struggle to **ask for help.** The lack of positive and healthy support often leads to feelings of being completely overwhelmed and this can further contribute to other mental and physical issues.

Lonely people have a poor quality of sleep.
As I have mentioned, sleep is vital and can bring out our creative bones.
Sleep helps with our memory and is a must for completing everyday tasks.

Effects of loneliness in the elderly

Many people *are* aware of how lonely elderly people can be.
The *effects* loneliness can have on elders on the other hand, is what many aren't aware of.

Lonely elders have higher levels of functional decline. Functional decline refers to the ability to do day-to-day activities, such as feeding themselves, walking, talking, and functioning without assistance.
This is because the immune systems of lonely elders are a lot more compromised than those that have healthy company.

It's clear that loneliness affects all people, regardless of age, sex, religion or location.
The effects can be severe, but also, loneliness does not just affect you (yeah *you, reading this right now)*, but it affects those that are very close to you.

Quality over Quantity

Truth be told, I was that kid described in the above paragraph on the effects of loneliness on children.

Growing up, I was a very lonely kid and viewed the world as a dangerous and scary place. I developed a lot of negative defense mechanisms; bad coping mechanisms.
I started losing all morals. I often lied, stole, and I started consuming alcohol from an early age.
As time went on, I discovered that I could use these bad coping mechanisms to my advantage.
I could use this to finally feel a part of and to fill that empty void, which was my feelings of loneliness.

Eventually, I had more friends than I could ever have imagined. The only problem, was that I still *felt* lonely. It wasn't long after that, that I came to realize that having a lot of company does not necessarily help with loneliness.
What really matters is having a few close, happy and healthy relationships.

When do people feel lonely?

We have gone through some of the main and most important reasons people feel lonely, but the reasons why people feel lonely differs from person to person.

- **After loss of a loved one**
  There is a deep silence when losing a loved one. Knowing that you will never hear their voice again or see the things that they used to do, which made them who they were. These people are often an integral part of our lives and when they are gone, we know that we will never get to experience their presence again.

- **Isolation**
  Wanting to spend quality alone time is good thing, but when you consistently spend extended periods of time alone, this is when you start feeling lonely.

- **Emotional isolation**
  It is possible for someone to be in a relationship with someone and still be emotionally shut off. This is often used as a defense mechanism to protect themselves and is because of insecurities, fears, or lack of self-confidence. This person *shuts down,* so they end up feeling lonely, even when they have people around.

- **Social phobia**
  This is also known as social anxiety disorder. Some people are scared of interactions that involve other people. They avoid social interactions at all costs and fear that they may be judged, misunderstood, or simply not fit in.

- **Social media**
  Social media is one of the biggest contributors to people feeling lonely. In this age of millennials, many people detract from life, as they feel more comfortable engaging online.

- **Depression**
  Depression is one of the biggest causes of loneliness. People that are depressed may form anxiety which makes it hard for them to interact with people, they may not be in the mood to be around people or they don't feel worthy of other's company.

- **Negativity**
  Constantly being negative can drive people away from you. Negative people often feel that people do not want to be around them or be there

for them and this is true. Nobody wants to be around somebody that constantly dampens their mood.

- **Hurt too many times – guard up**
  Some people have been hurt by others far too many times and as a result they are very untrusting and struggle to let people into their lives.

- **Unrealistic expectations**
  In my opinion, we all have expectations of others. We expect people to behave in a certain manner; we expect them to do certain things, to be respectful etc.
  A lot of people have completely unrealistic expectations of others, and when people do not live up to their expectations, they have failed.

Now that we have a better understanding of loneliness and how it affects us, let's go through a few things we can implement to treat loneliness.

How to deal with loneliness?

Quality relationships are not just when you're going through a rough patch and simply need a friend to dump all your problems onto.
Closeness with another, is a relationship that is mutually beneficial. We often feel lonely when we have problems and feel like we have no one to talk to.
Start by developing these healthy relationships before you get to the *problematic phase of loneliness,* to ensure that you are not simply using those close to you only when you're in need.

If you have existing relationships and when completely honest with yourself; you realize that you are probably not doing all that you can to ensure that these existing relationships are a success, then start by focusing on your existing relationships.
Don't go out looking. Focus on developing healthier and more positive relationships from your existing relationships before seeking out new ones.
Remember the quality over quantity rule.

Many people struggle to get to that stage of ensuring that their existing relationships are healthy and mutually beneficial, because they struggle to form these relationships in the first place.

Here are my below suggestions to fighting loneliness:

Volunteer
Volunteering can help fight loneliness. It is one of the most effective ways of dealing with loneliness. Not only do you feel a sense of connection, but you also

feel a sense of accomplishment, knowing that you have done good in the life of someone else today.

Dig deep
By now, I know, I've mentioned this a thousand times.
Be willing to dig deep and understand the root cause of your loneliness.
Are you perhaps expecting too much from people?
Have you been isolating, yet you wonder why nobody else has bothered to try to connect with you?
Have you started dealing with all the underlying issues that have prevented you from building healthy and substantial relationships?
Knowing that you're lonely is good, but understanding why you're lonely is another thing entirely. That knowledge grants you power, with that power, you know what areas need to be addressed.

Forgiveness
Many of us struggle to develop new and healthy relationships because we have been hurt in the past and we hold onto that resentment and hurt. Forgiveness is an essential tool in freeing yourself.

Positivity
People do not want to be around negative people. It's off-putting. If you fall into this category, perhaps you need to start implementing a positive, healthier outlook on life. Start actively seeking out the positive in every seemingly negative situation. Surround yourself with positive people; much like loneliness, positivity is contagious.

Comparing yourself to others
People are all born unique and as individuals. Stop comparing yourself to others. This is a self-defeating exercise and will only leave you feeling empty and lonelier than ever before. You will never have what someone else has and they will never have what you have.
Focus on the beauty of individuality, find your true place in this world and own it.

Sleep. Eat. Less stress.
Find healthy ways to manage stress. Develop healthy coping mechanisms. Stress can become so overwhelming that it will leave you feeling hopeless. When you're stressed out, you don't want to be around others, let alone seek help and support.
As mentioned, sleep is vital to our wellbeing. Without quality sleep, we cannot function at optimal levels. Ensure that you receive quality sleep every night.
A healthy diet is one of the most fundamental aspects of physical and mental wellbeing. By ensuring that you have a healthy diet, your confidence and esteem

levels are that much higher. This makes social engagement a lot more manageable.

Pay compliments

This may sound like the weirdest idea ever, but the simple act of paying random people honest and sincere compliments can help develop positive connections and you feel a lot more positive and better about yourself, knowing that you have contributed towards making someone else smile.

If all else fails, seek help

Unfortunately, dealing with loneliness is not easy. It is one of the most complex problems to deal with.
That being said, the above methods should help for a lot of people, but it may not help for all, especially not if you have severe psychological issues holding you back.
In these cases, I would recommend you see a professional psychologist or social worker that can help you develop healthy coping mechanisms, deal with the underlying problems around your loneliness and develop positive social skills.

Conclusion

Loneliness is a problem that affects many. It is a multi-layered problem that remains one of the most prominent and difficult to address.
The effects of loneliness can be very devastating, but there are available solutions to deal with loneliness.

Make sure that you are not looking to find happiness outside of yourself, but rather, ensure that you have started working on finding happiness from within. Once we can find happiness from within, we know our value, we know what we are worth and we know what we deserve.
Only then, do we start developing mutually healthy relationships.

CHAPTER TWENTY-TWO

The value of a smile

In "happy" situations, our natural bodily function would be to smile. This releases an incredible amount of those feel-good endorphins. To put this into perspective, smiling can release more happy endorphins than alcohol, drugs, or even chocolate. Powerful messages are sent to and from the brain and this ultimately uplifts even the dullest of moods. It instils in us positivity that can carry you out for the rest of the day.
The simple act of smiling can increase your overall mood, lower anxiety levels, lower stress levels; it can even help you look more attractive.

Because your mood is lifted, you feel lighter; less stressed, less overwhelmed and can assist you in experiencing an overall feeling of contentment.
Smiling actually increases your productivity, not only that, you become more approachable when you smile.
Your smile is contagious and others around you smile because of your smile.

Ever noticed how no matter how crappy your day may have been, when someone tells you a joke and you manage to break into a smile, you somehow feel better?

How can I possibly smile with so many bad things happening in my life right now?

Sometimes, nothing seems to be going right in your life. Days are dark. Friends may seem few. You have every reason to frown and very little to smile.

Smiling may seem like a natural bodily function when you're happy. Now, given all the benefits that smiling can bring, it may seem like you cannot benefit from all the good a smile can bring.

Making Progress

You may think that smiling only comes about when you actually have something to smile about.
If this sounds like you, then you're wrong.

It has been proven that "forcing" a smile can lead you to feel better.
Forcing a smile can assist by reducing stress levels, it can instil in us a sense of gratitude and uplift your overall mood.

No matter how good or bad your day may seem.
Try and smile, you will be surprised at just how beneficial it will be.
A simple smile can brighten not only your day, but those around you.

The value of a smile…

It's late Saturday evening in the city that never sleeps. Catherine was found slaving away at CNA, a local bookstore.
Not that she minded, she loved it. It gave her extra income and she got to read plenty of books without having to pay. Working late and ungodly hours had never been an issue for her. Besides, she needed the money. With unparalleled exotic elegance and beauty, she never knew if all these men actually had a genuine interest in stationery, literary pieces, or if they were just trying to get in her pants.
In any case, she was not interested in any them.

Not after the hell she's been through.

A smile can tell a million stories. A glum mood can be lifted, a deal is struck, a person's confidence may be boosted, or an apology is accepted. A smile can cover hurt. It can cover pain. A smile can hide anger, remorse, and resentment. A smile can, even if it's just for that moment, lead you to believe that everything will be okay.

She smiles.
"Hi there, need help?"

CHAPTER TWENTY-THREE

A compliment a day keeps the psychiatrist away

We live in a very self-consumed world. Life has become one big competition and, let's face it, competition is rife.
People competing with each other, each wanting to look better than the next, wanting to have a better looking spouse, more money, fancier, and bigger material possessions than everyone else.
Happiness is increasingly being measured by the amount of material and superficial possessions we have. It's little wonder that the amount of lonely people is at a staggering all-time high.

Studies show that 20% of the total world's population is lonely or experiences symptoms of loneliness. This very loneliness is what drives people to addiction or other obsessive, unhealthy activities.

Loneliness can either directly or indirectly be attributed to the fact that people have lost that "connection" with others.
With all the competition in today's world, it's easy to understand how people are starting to lose that "connection."

Many of us, including myself, are so consumed in themselves that they fail to see value in everything else around us.
By consumed, I mean *being consumed in my own little world; where I am in life, how well I am doing, what makes me happy.* It's little wonder that I started to lose that very important connection with others.

A complimentary study

I decided to try out a little experiment on the value of paying someone a compliment – a complimentary study on the value of a compliment. Excuse the pun.
Paying someone an honest compliment involved me thinking about someone other than myself, it forced me to get out of my head and think about the value of those around me. In doing so, I would hopefully see the beauty in others.

The little study was that for a week, I would try and pay five compliments, five honest and sincere compliments. I was not allowed to go to bed that night until I had paid them all.
If the compliment felt insincere, it didn't count; I had to keep looking for opportunities, until I genuinely paid someone a compliment.
At the end of the week, I would gauge and see if I had experienced anything unusual or different.

Actively going out there and looking for nice things to say, felt a bit strange at first, but once I got the hang of it, it almost became normal.

"I really like your dress."
"You must be one of the smartest people I have ever come across."
"Heaven must be missing an angel, because I am looking at one."

Okay, the last line was just a really bad pick-up line, but you get my drift.

The results I experienced were incredible.
People are very receptive to honest, sincere compliments and you can tell that your simple gesture made their day.
A glum mood is contagious as is a happy mood. When you randomly pay someone a compliment, their mood is automatically lifted and that rubs off on you.

If you want others to like you, if you want to develop real friendships, if you want to help others at the same time as you help yourself, keep this principle in mind: Become genuinely interested in other people. – Dale Carnegie.

What really stood out for me was that by genuinely taking an interest in someone else, I started feeling good about myself for having noticed the beauty and value others. Their smiles made me smile.

Final thoughts:
A simple act of paying another a compliment has been amazing, not only for others, but for myself as well.
Intentionally focusing on paying others a compliment has proven to be very helpful. Actively thinking about others, other than myself has been very uplifting and I felt a definite sense of connectedness with others.
Overall, the experiment proved to be a great success to myself.

About the Author

Know the rules, then break them.

Brady Moller is an author. Born in 1990 and currently lives in Johannesburg, South Africa.
As a recovering addict, he learned many of life's lessons at a very young age and now spends a lot of his time working on his mental wellness and addiction site: http://www.eyesofanaddict.com, as well as realizing his dream by writing both fiction and non-fiction.
He specifically enjoys writing about everyday issues people are faced with. Bringing these issues to light are crucial for the success of our society at large.

I would like to thank you for taking the time to read this book and if you enjoyed this read, I would truly appreciate an Amazon review with your feedback.
Furthermore, I want nothing less than to offer my loyal readers my new and upcoming books either free or at the lowest available price possible.
I LOVE nothing more than connecting with my readers. I would love to hear your thoughts, insights, or even suggestions. Pop me an email at brady@eyesofanaddict.com
You can also be added to my mailing list and be the first to know about any new releases. The other advantage is that you will also be the first to know on any promotions for my upcoming novels.

Be sure to subscribe to be the first to know when any upcoming books are set for release.

[Subscribe to the mailing list by clicking here!](#)

Be sure to check out my website as well, there's some really cool self-help stuff you will definitely enjoy, and hopefully, it may be of a lot of use to you and someone you're close to.

For more on the author, check out his website
www.eyesofanaddict.com

Be sure to subscribe and follow Brady Moller on Amazon:
http://www.amazon.com/author/bradymoller

Finally, your book reviews on Amazon mean the world to me, they help me pursue my dream of writing, and would be truly appreciated.

Stay blessed.
Brady Moller.

Made in the USA
Coppell, TX
05 May 2020